The Ghosts of Charleston

The
Ghosts
of
Charleston

Edward B. Macy

Julian T. Buxton III

Beaufort Books ✦ New York

First Edition

Library of Congress Cataloging-in-Publication Data
Buxton, Julian T. III, 1961–
    The ghosts of Charleston / Julian T. Buxton III, Edward B.
        Macy.— 1st ed.
        p.cm.
    Includes bibliographical references.
    ISBN 0-8253-0505-5
    1. Ghosts — South Carolina — Charleston. I.
Macy, Edward. II. Title

BF1472.U6 B89 2000
133.1'09757'915 — dc21   00-048573

Published in the United States by Beaufort Books,
New York, New York

Modern photos by William Struhs except those on pages 4, 50, 68, 83, 101, and 145, which are the work of Laurens Smith.
Photo on page 134 copyright © South Carolina Historical Society.
All rights reserved.

10   9   8   7   6   5   4   3   2

Printed in the United States of America

In Memory
of
Mickey Meads

✦ ✦ ✦

To Shannon
— E.B.M.

✦

To Carol M. Graf, M.D.
— J.T.B.

Very far from myself I come toward you

In the fire of the sun, dead-locked
With the moon's new face in its glory.
I see by the dark side of light.
I am he who I should have become.
A bird that has died overhead
Sings a song to sustain him forever.
Elsewhere I have dreamed of my birth,
And come from my death as I dreamed;

Each time the moon has burned backward.
Each time, my heart has gone from me
And shaken the sun from the moonlight.
Each time, a woman has called,
And my breath come to life in her singing.
Once more I come home from my ghost.

— James Dickey
From *Into the Stone*

Contents

Introduction

There are so many ghosts in Charleston that I find it difficult to breathe at night while walking down the overgrown alleys and lamp lit streets, or just sitting on the Battery gazing at the green and white harbor lights, listening to the waves. The air is deathly thick with them. You don't really walk about Charleston, you wade through its air.

Sometimes late at night you can hear the ghosts moaning in great groups. Those are the most disturbing. But also you can hear little girls murmuring and laughing, then scrambling away down a dark alley or up the worn stairs of a huge old planter's mansion. What is very rare, but unforgettable, are the ones that blow the hot wet air through your hair and then yell out and echo far down an otherwise still, quiet street, streaking chaos until their madness suddenly reaches a pitch and then drowns in the harbor's dark calm.

The daytime is not as bad as all this, but then, no matter how engaged I am, I can never forget the nights.

> — *Excerpt from a letter to a friend,*
> *October 11, 1990*

I wrote the above five years before I ever imagined there would be a Ghosts of Charleston walking tour or *The Ghosts of Charleston* book. At the time I lived in Malibu, California, purposefully making my home in an American culture and geography as far removed from Charleston as possible. I taught humanities at Pepperdine University for a short while. The rest of the time I read and wrote in a cabin on the top of Las Flores Canyon.

This Malibu cabin sat nearly 2,000 feet above the ocean. Because of Lowcountry flatness, such a perspective is not possible in Charleston. At twenty-eight years of age I stood on the sundeck of my new home and declared success: I had made my way in Los Angeles culture. I had cut myself off from my roots, detached myself from my origins, and thereby achieved freedom. So I thought.

For me, California silenced Charleston's siren call. For fourteen years after high school I ran from all that Charleston meant and was to me. In Malibu, I thought I was free from it but I was not. The fact is at the age of thirty-three I realized Charleston's beauty and tradition continued to smother me.

The city's magnetic pull was constant even through all of the marvelously distracting wonders — and terrors — of living in southern California. For example, whenever I returned to the city for a college break, or for a visit from California, my mind slowed. Everything became thick and distorted. I could not think straight. At night, strange deja vu feelings and visions from the 1700s and 1800s flashed through me, making it difficult just to take a simple stroll down Church Street.

I am no longer haunted in such ways. I returned to Charleston in early 1994, and faced the siren's call.

A student of mine sent me a copy of my 1990 letter. She had seen me on *Haunted History,* the show Ed Macy, my colleague, and I produced with the History Channel in 1998, and remembered my letter.

She began her letter saying that she was happy to see me in my present employment. She then wrote that, "laced through all your class discussions was the obvious fact that you were running from ghosts of various sorts from life in your home city. This is an example of true poetic justice. You now have these ghosts working for you. . . ."

Living in Charleston is now a joy. The resolution to my dilemma came through finding a way to embrace what happens to my imagination when I live here. Rather than to be paralyzed by it, employ it. As a result of this decision, every day, through Tour Charleston LLC, the business Ed Macy and I operate, stories about happenings from Charleston's rich past are kept alive.

Resolution also came from writing this book. These stories are not about my personal ghosts. Rather, the stories collected here are born of events experienced on the fringes of Charleston's collective psyche. What Ed and I have done is to collect a vast amount of information through research and countless interviews with Charlestonians, and to form that information into this book of ghost stories.

Charlestonians have always known that Charleston abounds with supernatural activity. Because of the reverence we feel toward Charleston, we felt strongly that our stories be appropriate to the character and integrity of the city. Charlestonians are sometimes accused of taking themselves and their heritage too seriously. Ghost stories are certainly meant to be entertaining. But the fact is that the experiences described in this book are real. They are not hokey events out of our imaginations. What exactly these ghosts and the experiences surrounding them are — entities from the underworld, or eventually scientifically explainable events — I do not know.

The criterion established for the stories was that several people had experienced the same bizarre occurrences in the same location over and over again. Ed and I then wove their stories into historical context.

We hope you find these stories entertaining. But more than that we hope that you experience a piece of what we felt while writing them — an interaction with mystery and wonder.

Julian Buxton
October 2000

The Ghosts of Charleston

The Aiken-Rhett House

At 10 P.M. on August 12, 1989, architects Eddie Fava and Reggie Gibson proceeded across the expansive double drawing rooms on the first floor of the great Aiken-Rhett House. Through the dark they advanced toward the primary entrance and the three-story high marble stairwell.

Both of them were fatigued from a long day of hard work, and ready for sleep. Their intention was to complete one last piece of work, a routine request made by Sonitrol, the company in charge of the mansion's security system.

The massive structure stood dark and quiet, framed only by stars and a moonless sky.

Originally constructed in 1817, the Aiken-Rhett occupies the length of an entire city block. All but two basement rooms exist without electricity. Because preservationists have chosen to leave it unrestored, the house presents an unusually menacing aspect, even in daylight. At night the Aiken-Rhett turns into a huge dead space, a towering black giant that dominates the entire neighbor-hood.

That summer Fava and Gibson measured the whole house, its every feature, including even the trim. Their work established an official Historical American Building Survey (HABS). These HABS drawings documented their findings for present day study and preserved archi-tectural knowledge intact for future generations.

Up until this late summer day, nothing out of the ordinary had transpired. But at ten minutes until 10 P.M., Sonitrol monitors detected wind blowing through the second floor ballroom. They notified Fava and Gibson, and asked them to close the windows in that room before locking the doors for the night.

After that, nothing more was ordinary. The young architects approached the central stairway. Upon step-ping on the first stair, a shrill, high-pitched noise flooded their hearing. Both men covered their ears. When they reached the midpoint between floors, a loud whirring noise shook the stairwell and grew louder from behind the door of the second floor ballroom.

As they approached the rattling door, the disparate sounds increased in pitch over a period of several seconds until both dropped tone and merged into one constant roar as loud as a freight train.

When Gibson touched the doorknob, all sound and movement ceased. He opened the door to find a perfect-ly sealed room — no open windows, no wind blowing. Throughout the once magnificent ballroom, all was still and quiet. They walked past the louvered piazza doors, past the long, gilded mirror centered against the far wall, and continued deep into the heart of the room.

With eyes wide and shifting in all directions, neither of them spoke. Fava beamed his flashlight all around the room. Nothing was there.

Then both men saw it: a distinct movement through the room. Something was there, not a reflection. They felt it glide by, then saw motion behind them in the mirror.

Fava wheeled, casting his light around, again seeing nothing but wood floors and tattered wallpaper.

Both men stood absolutely still. Coming from the direction of the mirror was the sound of sustained, heavy sobbing. As they turned, the sobbing stopped. But in that mirror glared an intense, wide-eyed old woman. Strands of her long white hair rose and snapped in a breeze that Fava and Gibson could not feel.

She gathered energy into her face and body through a deep inhalation. She then put her hands to the sides of her head and bent into a scream so long and hard that her whole body shook.

She wailed in absolute silence.

The Aiken-Rhett House does not exist as a pristine restored example of antebellum affluence nor as a sentimental object representing faded southern glamour. It is intact and preserved, a rare time capsule of domestic architecture and social history, but it is not restored. Yet one of antebellum America's richest and most powerful families lived there. The site remained in one family from 1826 until 1975.

William Aiken Sr. (1779–1831) arrived in Charleston from Northern Ireland in 1789 at age eleven. By age twenty-one he was already a prosperous cotton merchant. For the next thirty-two years Aiken vastly increased his wealth through cotton enterprises and real estate investments. He served in the state legislature for the last eight years of his life.

Probably the best example of his visionary thinking and entrepreneurial acumen was his work in founding the state's first rail venture, and the world's largest under one management, the South Carolina Canal and Railway Company. On the tracks of this company ran *The Best*

During the HGTV production in June 2000, a reenactment of carriages arriving for a ball held at the Aiken-Rhett House.

Friend, the first passenger locomotive to be used in a business venture in the United States.

After the death of William Aiken, Sr. in 1831, William Aiken, Jr. (1806–1887) and his wife Harriet Lowndes (1812–1892) selected this house to be their residence from the senior Aiken's many real estate holdings. They drew plans and gave orders for extensive renovations.

Then, in 1833, the young couple set sail for New York and a grand tour of Europe. They purchased furnishings for their new home: expensive furniture, crystal and brass chandeliers from Paris, black marble mantels, fine works of art including marble statuary acquired in Florence and Rome, and several gilt-framed mirrors.

Harriet Lowndes Aiken, whose life-sized portrait still hangs in the east drawing room, experienced the beauty, grandeur and riches of the antebellum South as much as any woman of her time. At one point she and her husband owned over 700 slaves, making them one of the largest individual slaveholders in South Carolina.

The value of the slaves alone put the Aikens among the very top echelon of rich southern families. Many of their slaves lived and worked on their giant rice plantation Jehossee, near Edisto Island. Yet, a full twenty house servants and groundkeepers lived on the estate at 48 Elizabeth Street under the immediate service of William, Jr. and Harriet. These slaves also catered to the needs of the frequent guests and made possible the extravagant meals and grand balls for which the Aikens were well known.

On festive nights, guests arrived by carriage at the side entrance, the house full of people and merry conversation. Laughter and music filled the air. Gas and candlelit chandeliers flooded yellow light through the dozens of windows.

In 1839 Francis Kinloch Middleton attended a ball at the house shortly after the completion of the first renovations.

> Last night I was at the handsomest ball I have ever seen — given by Mrs. Aiken — they live . . . in a house he had added to and furnished very handsomely — the 2 floors were entirely thrown open —

The ballroom.

the orchestra from the theatre played for the dancers — and the supper table was covered with a rich service of silver — lights in profusion, and a crowded, handsomely dressed assembly . . .

— *From the Letters of Francis Kinloch Middleton*

Precious little is known about the intimate personal details of the lives of William and Harriet Aiken. What is known is that the couple lived unusually public lives. Besides William, Jr.'s achievements as a businessman and

Harriet Lowndes Aiken.

plantation owner, he also served in the state legislature (1838–1844), as Governor of South Carolina (1844–1846), and in the U.S. House of Representatives (1851–1857) where he served as Speaker of the House in 1855.

The Aikens entertained the rich and famous of their times. On the evening of November 28, 1863, Confederate President Jefferson Davis enjoyed an enthusiastic reception at 48 Elizabeth Street. According to diarist Mary Boykin Chesnut,

> Governor Aiken's perfect old Carolina style of living delighted [Davis]. Those old gray-haired darkies and their noiseless, automatic service, the result of finished training — one does miss that sort of thing when away from home, where your own servants think for you; they save you from all responsibility even in matters of your own ease and well doing.

It is uncertain what the slaves thought of all this. There is no surviving documentation recording their impressions. What is certain is that the Aikens seemed to live the epitome of the romanticized southern life.

In 1865 that lifestyle came to a crashing halt. Charleston lay in bombed-out ruins. Visitors to the city after the war depict a mournful spectacle. The once bustling wharves were rotting; the churches, homes and public highways were filled with gaping holes from the federal shelling; and a whole section of town was reduced to ashes by the many fires.

J. T. Trowbridge, touring the South after the war, wrote that the ruins of Charleston were the "most picturesque of any I saw in the South." He noted that in the worst sections:

> Broad, semicircular flights of marble steps, leading up once to broad doorways, now conduct you over their cracked and calcined slabs, to the level of high foundations swept of everything but their former superstructures . . . Above the monotonous gloom of the ordinary ruins rise the churches, — the stone tower and roofless walls of the Catholic Cathedral, deserted and solitary, a roost for buzzards.

Whereas the Great Fire of 1861 decimated the upper part of the city, and contributed most to its gloomy appearance, the federal bombardment performed its work in shattering many beautiful planters' residences in the lower section.

Every account written of Charleston after the Civil War describes the citizens of the battered city as utterly despondent. Whitelaw Reid, another writer touring the south after the war, called it a "City of Desolation." Sidney Andrews wrote after observing the citizens of Charleston, "Here is enough woe and want and ruin to satisfy the most insatiate heart . . ."

In the lower sections South of Broad Street the stillness of death and desertion reigned. Many veterans returning to their families and homes — what they believed to be their only solaces in such miserable times — stood heartbroken at their own front steps on finding their destroyed homes now filled with former slave families.

General William T. Sherman himself said that

"Anyone who is not satisfied with war should go and see Charleston, and he will pray louder and deeper than ever that the country may in the long future be spared of any more war."

Farther up the peninsula, the Aiken-Rhett House survived the war intact. Although the Aikens were by no means penniless, the primary vehicle for their earnings, the Agricultural System, no longer existed. In 1874 the proud Aikens petitioned the U.S. government to be reimbursed for their significant economic losses. In it they listed the names of some of their domestic slaves:

> Ann Greggs and her son Henry Greggs, Sambo and his wife Dorcas Richardson and her children Charles, Rachael, Victoria, Elizabeth and Julia, Charles Jackson and Anthony Barnwell, and two carpenters Will and Jacob.

They included these slaves "in and about [their] family" and "of [their] immediate household." The government refused to recognize the legitimacy of the Aikens' claim to human property and denied them reimbursement for their losses.

William and Harriet Aiken represent archetypal personalities for American historical literature. Much is made of them as real historical personages whose opulent lifestyles grow evermore romantic through the mind's eye. Yet, the less romantic and less remembered postbellum period of their lives contributes just as significantly to understanding American history and the effects of extreme economic and psychological loss.

The east drawing room.

William and Harriet both lived for over twenty years after the end of the Civil War, enduring their great personal and economic losses with dignity. After William died in 1887, Harriet transformed the second floor ballroom, making it into a comforting, spacious bedroom.

She lived there in the same room where, from 1835–1865, she had orchestrated a social center stage for American elite. However, after William's death except for her routine daily movements and those of her servants, that magnificent ballroom, once so full of abundance and life, stood dead still for five years. There was plenty of quiet time for Harriet Lowndes Aiken to feel the loss of her husband and to retrace those last three glorious decades of opulent Southern life.

Harriet Aiken died in 1892. After her death, Henrietta Aiken Rhett (1836–1918), Harriet's daughter, locked the ballroom door. It remained sealed until 1974, like a time capsule, closed and unused for eighty-two years.

Harriet lived to experience the sharp decline of the massive Aiken-Rhett family resources. Any hope for a return to glory for the great house evaporated when it passed out of the hands of the Aiken-Rhett family in 1975. Frances Dill Rhett (1882–1982), Henrietta's daughter-in-law and the last of the line to live in the house, donated it to the Charleston Museum. By that time, the house was in sad shape. All but four rooms, lived in by Frances and a servant, remained sealed off.

Today the great house stands silent. The only sound emanating from its once joy and wonder filled corridors comes from respectful docents. In the eager but hushed tones of the museum reverent, they tell of the glory days of William and Harriet Aiken. All the while, the eyes of Harriet, full of regal dignity both serene and intense, endure the numbing stillness from the life-size drawing room portrait. From there she regards those who come day after day, year after year, to hear about the life she lived.

On some evenings the years come and weigh on the spirit of the house. Memories drop into its rooms and shades of happenings long ago pass along its walls. The great releases of spirit into the material world no longer exist: no glorified trips to Europe, no bountiful party splendor. The pressure between what is and what was intensifies.

Release comes. From the depths of the ballroom, shut to the world for eighty-two years, emerges a spirit that rages against the fading of a lifetime of material wonder and power.

East Bay Specter

In the unlikely setting of Charleston's busy East Bay Street exists the city's most visually arresting specter. Its tilting head and bulging eyes flash out of windows and sweep a wide arc through the expansive third floor of the Wagener Building.

Late one evening in the summer of 1983, James McAlister III, manager at the popular East Bay Trading Company restaurant, prepared to close the upstairs bar. The kitchen had been shut down hours before; the only bodies remaining in the place were his staff and seven visiting employees from other restaurants already closed for the night. They relaxed with beer and cigarettes, telling stories, easing tensions built up during a busy night of work.

Tall windows encircle all three cavernous floors of the Wagener Building. The third floor provides panoramic views overlooking the harbor. Yet, the spectacular glass in this place makes for one drawback — it sometimes becomes hot as a greenhouse on the third floor. Sunshine radiates through the glass panels all day, baking the brick walls like an oven.

In the midst of the cheerful chatter and goodwill of that steamy July night, a deathly chill emanated from the south wall of the third floor. A few women crossed their arms and rubbed their hands along their cold skin. Obviously annoyed, they looked around for someone to turn off the air conditioning.

McAlister, puzzled by the sudden temperature change, walked over to the only air conditioning vent, a large blower in the center of the room by the elevator shaft. There, as well as in all other areas of the room except for the south wall, the air was as thick and steamy as ever.

By the time McAlister returned to the tables, the chill had become a persistent wall of wind blowing straight out of the brick. He later described it as feeling like an arctic blast, "like standing in a biting winter wind on the High Battery seawall."

The spectral wind blew for nearly ten minutes. At the peak of it, two waitresses seated near McAlister bent their heads away from the cold as their long blond hair blew horizontal to the table.

At the same time, a ship horn blared, vibrating loudly through the room. High above them, weak lighting from an unidentifiable source sparked and popped, partially illuminating the rafters with a weird, intermittent glow.

Two people shrieked and cowered in their chairs. They pointed long fingers toward something in the rafters.

McAlister threw his head back and looked up. The eerie glow faded. He saw nothing but heavy wood beams and darkness stretching high up into the overhang.

Several months later, a similar group relaxed on the third floor after a busy Friday night. The cold breeze blew again. This time it was not accompanied by the odd lighting above.

But when McAlister and his staff returned the next day to prepare for business, a stunning sight awaited them. The third floor furniture, normally lined in fine balance and symmetry, stood piled high in a chaotic mess.

The barstools and dozens of chairs, turned at all angles, made one huge mound in the corner along the south wall. The heavy wood tables, some of them built to accommodate eight to ten people, sat precariously high, well out of reach of even a tall man. At the very top, a large captain's chair slowly rocked in the center of the breezeless upper atmosphere. The seat of it balanced delicately on the legs of a mid-size table.

As the staff gathered in soundless awe around the top of the stairs across the room from the rocking captain's chair, the manager approached the tall heap. When he closed to within ten yards of the mound, the chair suddenly launched off its perch, traveling with force right at him. It dropped at his feet, splintering in pieces just inches away.

F. W. Wagener constructed his building at 161 East Bay Street in 1880 to house his expanding firm's wide-ranging enterprises. The property also included a three-story warehouse on Queen Street behind the main building. The warehouse featured 80 x 260 foot open floor spaces on each level. The combined warehouse and retail/office space bolstered an already dynamic business.

On the main building's first floor, F. W. Wagener & Co. sold marine supplies, as well as liquor and wholesale groceries. Yet, it was the cotton and fertilizer brokering offices on the upper two floors that made the Wagener firm rich.

South Carolina's economy boomed in the last two decades of the 1800s. Money poured into the state from England and the North to build what became the most powerful textile industry in the nation. But what enabled the textile industry to thrive was the hugely profitable phosphate business in Charleston. Phosphate mining created abundant and cheap fertilizer that Charlestonians sold to farmers everywhere.

With this fertilizer, South Carolina farmers produced record crops of cotton. Over time, cotton prices fell steadily. Farmers soon found themselves in the strange position of being surrounded by money in the form of phosphate and textile businessmen, and more cotton than ever, but their incomes declined.

It was in this economic environment that the scion of a prosperous antebellum planter and merchant family found himself in dire psychological and financial straits. George Poirier, a client of the Wagener firm, based his self-worth on social status and the accomplishments of his ancestors. In his case, building his integrity on such a fragile foundation proved to be lethal.

From 1861 to 1865, the Poirier family contributed a significant portion of their financial power to the Confederate cause. Yet, like many of Charleston's business elite, they hedged their bets by shrewdly (and quietly) diversifying their investments outside the Confederate economy. They invested in British companies and United States bonds.

The result was that after the Civil War, the core of the Poirier family fortune remained intact. Instead of having to face the abject poverty that many once well-to-do Charleston families confronted, young George inherited a working cotton plantation, and ample cash resources to run it.

Yet for George, the success of his ancestors created a burden they never imagined or intended. Never challenged by having dirt on his hands or by having to build character through his own accomplishments, George lacked business instinct. His unearned status and pride blunted his capacity to make good decisions.

In his case, the problem was worse than that. As energetic and likeable as he was on the outside, he felt tortured inside by a vague but driving sense of guilt and insecurity. The same energy that drove his forebears to ruthlessly flesh out economic success drove him to relentless madness and despair. The weight of tradition began to smother him; everyday living became a strain.

Later some speculated that there had not been enough value sharpening trial by fire in his life. Others believed it was a case of bad genes, that insanity was a secret Poirier family affliction. Whatever the case, it is likely that George had avoided the hard task of developing his own set of values. For George Poirier, the cherished value system of his high society Charleston peers, with its aristocratic disdain for hard work and its emphasis on past family accomplishments, proved to be a foundation of sand in the face of financial and psychological destruction.

Starting in 1885, Charleston merchants enjoyed a strong, yet brief, economic boom from the mining of phosphate for fertilizer. By then George Poirier had run through his inheritance and had taken out a mortgage on his land.

He had alienated his wife and run off many of his best employees and field hands. In the weeks before his total financial ruin, George's behavior became disturbingly erratic. According to the reports of neighbors, he alternated between catatonic depressions and raving tanrums. In the fields, he was heard screaming wild, incomprehensible orders at field hands. Then, only seconds later, he could be seen darting from vegetable bin to cotton bale, twisting samples in the sun, and laughing with stunning ferocity.

Boll weevil infestation brought the penultimate blow. The cotton-eating vermin destroyed most of his crop. His employees wrested as much good cotton from the diseased fields as possible. Late one afternoon, George transported his sparse cotton load to town, checked it in at the docks, and arranged with the brokers at the Wagener office for a ship to take it that night.

His plan was to live off the profit of this last load,

keep creditors at bay, and invest it in the speculative stock of one of the booming start-up phosphate businesses. To his distorted thinking, all hope of upholding some shell of the honorable Poirier family pride and tradition depended on this one shipment.

As the sun set and the last of the brokers left their Wagener Building offices for home, George remained. Next to a tall third floor window, he sat in a wide captain's chair and stared out over the steel blue harbor water. The ship carrying his payload steamed out of port toward the Atlantic. As he watched it with rapt intensity, he pondered the journey the vessel would make across the sea with the remnant of his once proud fortune. Then an awful sight slapped him from his reverie. By the time the ship reached the far end of the harbor, an excessive amount of heavy smoke trailed from its stern. His heart raced. Surely, it is issuing from the stacks, he reasoned. Moments later his mouth went dry; a sweaty chill tingled on his scalp and neck. Smoke was billowing from the windows near the waterline. George stood, face and hands pressed against the glass, his hot breath fogging his view.

On board the ship, a rum drunken sailor smoking a pipe had fallen asleep in the hold of the ship, amidst hundreds of bales of Lowcountry cotton. The last thing George saw from the top windows of the Wagener Building was the ship, fully engulfed in flames, sailors leaping from her deck as she burned down to the waterline and sunk.

Exactly what goes on inside a person's head in the

moments before he commits to executing himself? What extreme degree of psychic torture ignites the decision to end all opportunities for healing in this world? Is it better to take the chance in the great unknown — a place where there may be even fewer opportunities to emancipate oneself from hell? No man can say. What is known is that suicide is the ultimate no return, the final act in *this* world.

George Poirier positioned his chair under one of the long rafter beams above him. He tied a baling line around his neck. He could feel the pressure of his jugular veins pumping against the coarse rope. He then lashed the other end over the exposed beam and tied it off. Without hesitation, he kicked out the chair. His neck snapped back, and George Poirier flew into cold galaxies beyond.

As the sun's rays broke over the harbor the next morning, a crowd drew around a newspaper delivery boy who had gone berserk. Old men shopkeepers tried to calm him; his screams were unintelligible. He kicked his legs and threw his hands in front of his face until a kind man gently wrapped his arms around him.

"What is it, boy?"

The child slowly looked up and pointed west toward the corner of East Bay and Queen Streets. At first, the crowd saw nothing to cause alarm. But as a lone sunbeam broke free from a passing cloud, it lit up the glass all along East Bay Street. High in the Wagener Building dangled the long silhouette of a hanged man.

As the ray shifted with the rising sun, other dark shadows joined the silhouette. Before another cloud obscured the figures in the window, a gruesome spectacle became clear. Large birds had flown in through an open window. They pecked with force at the eyes and face of the twisting body.

The modern architects who remodeled the site wisely left the wide-open spaces of Wagener's original floor plan intact. Visitors today will not see a contorted heap of tables and chairs. Nor is it likely they will find hungry falcons trapped in the high roofing. But from time to time, a cold breeze blows straight out of the brick wall on the third floor. And whether lit from an unexplainable weird glow inside, or from a stormy bolt of lightening outside, the dangling silhouette of a hanged man still flashes through the rafters of the Wagener Building's third floor.

The Garden Theatre

Many Charleston specters have tried to intimidate Wade Kersey in the past. As the jack-of-all-trades at the Dock Street Theatre, Wade has encountered many supernatural experiences in the building. He is almost immune to bizarre, inexplicable phenomena. Perhaps this nonchalance comes from being numbed from overexposure. Or possibly, it is a natural result of Marine Corps combat during the Gulf War. Yet, none of this prepared Wade for a shocking experience he had in another of Charleston's esteemed theatres.

The Garden Theatre is located on the upper end of King Street, very close to Calhoun Street. The "King of Charleston Theatre," Albert Sottile, built it toward the end of World War I. It originally featured Vaudeville acts and some of the city's first moving pictures.

A common sight in southern cities for most of the twentieth century was the "Colored Entrance" sign that hung over the less prominent doorways of buildings. In the days before civil rights overtook the shadows of bla-

tant racism in the south, the Black community was subjugated to back balcony seating in movie theaters as well as most other public buildings.

This may help to explain the specter Wade encountered in the summer of 1994. He was setting up the theatre for a performance one afternoon, when he sensed he was not alone in the spacious, dimly lit building. He called out and got no response. Thinking one of King Street's many transients had broken into the building, Wade grabbed a long flashlight and walked through the floor level seating. In the fifth row sat a Black man of medium build, staring intently at his inquisitor.

Wade shouted, "Hey! What are you doing here?"

The gentleman looked back at him, seeming a bit confused.

Before he got an answer, Wade was stunned by a furious flurry of sight, sound, and air. This Black fellow, who had been sitting only a few feet away from Wade, shot up into the balcony, landing in the furthest row of seats in the theatre, in an elapsed time of less than a tenth of a second, as if fired from some ectoplasmic cannon.

Ashen faced and terror stricken, Wade dropped his flashlight and rushed for the door. He broke into sunlight and fresh air, grateful for the ordinary site of busy King Street.

This specter is a grim reminder of Charleston's racially inharmonious past, another unfortunate spirit trapped in a pocket of time. When authority in the form of a surprised Wade Kersey confronted this lingering spirit, his afterlife instinct moved him back to where he sat during his lifetime.

The Legacy of Raymond Putnam Hill

In *My Family of Souls*, a book published in 1974, six years before he died, the successful engineer and international industrialist Raymond Putnam Hill foretold of a future incarnation in Charleston. During this next lifetime, scheduled to commence in 2043, Hill will take up residence in Charleston and live, once again, in the three-story brick single-house he restored at 12 Wentworth Street.

Hill died in 1980. Concerning his activities and whereabouts during this present "discarnate period," the book provides only the most general information. But people living in the house since his death have no doubt where he is: the discarnate soul of Raymond Putnam Hill exists in the house at 12 Wentworth Street, actively protecting its interests, and actively preparing for its imminent incarnation.

Raymond Hill's career fused engineering and science with shrewd business sense. He was born on September 12, 1888, in Springfield, Massachusetts. Hill spent much of his youth building and experimenting with mechanical and electrical devices. While only a teenager, he prospered as an electrical contractor. From then until he retired in 1956, Hill concentrated his work energies through several companies, two of which he formed. The first was Wolf and Hill, consultants in electrical engineering. The second one, which he ran for thirty-five years, was the Pulp Bleaching Corporation, which made machinery for commercial bleaching. During this time he designed and implemented over 100 electrical installations in countries throughout the world.

His success in business and technical enterprises demonstrates that the man was a realist, firmly planted in the physical world. Yet, he recognized as early as eight years old that he possessed special psychic talents. Some proved immediately practical. For instance, many times a "Voice" gave him detailed beneficent guidance. The first time, when he was only eleven years old, saved his life:

These manifestations were a startling illusion of actual sound coming to my ears from outside. One afternoon in August of 1899 I was passing the main switchboard in the power plant of which my father was in charge and heard a jingling sound that was not normal, and I soon traced it to a loose nut on one of the devices. This was a high-voltage terminal, but I was standing on a dry hardwood floor and knew I could safely tighten the nut with my bare hands. With the loose nut and its washer firmly in my fingers, I still heard a jingle and then noted that the opposite terminal was loose . . . I shifted tightening the first terminal to my left hand and reached for the other with my right. When I was within an inch of making what would have been a fatal contact, a strong voice seemed to shout into my ear, "Don't."

Early on Hill experienced frequent waking dreams. In later years he determined them to be accurate retrocognitive visions.

> I would see pictures of persons I knew to be I in various settings that were clearly of another age. These sometimes were stills, sometimes movies. Some… appeared only once, others again and again. There was no apparent order to these scenes… I appeared in two different embodiments, one a woman of the white race, the other a dark-skinned male.
> — From My *Family of Souls*

His book describes in vivid detail a panoply of psychic experience: visual perception of elementals ("semi-intelligent entities [that] do not incarnate in physical matter as we know it, but exist in a field that . . . permits them to be seen in a primitive state of clairvoyance . . . doubtless the basis of the many folk tales of 'little people' [referred to] in several cultures") as well as telesthetic perception of distant events.

Probably the most fascinating tale is Hill's summary of his life-long exploration into past and future lives. Most of such psychic research performed by Hill involved a personalized method of rhabdomancy, a divination practice once limited to search for water and other underground resources. Unlike the use of sticks or coins with oracles such as the *I Ching*, or cards in the case of tarot, this particular practice employs the use of a pendulum.

A more popular term for the divination practice Hill employed is "information dowsing." Over a period of decades Hill honed his pendulum reading skills and devised a more scientific method of obtaining information beyond the standard human senses. The authors of this book will not try to explain exactly how Hill

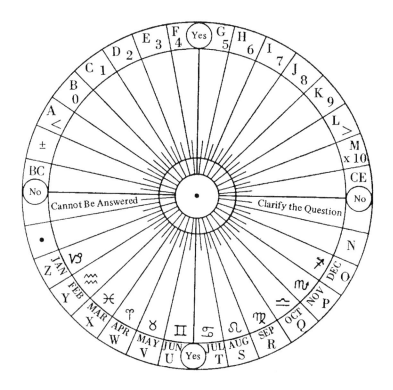

The rhabdomancy chart.

employed this unusual mechanism, nor could we even attempt the more difficult proposition of explaining Hill's remarkably detailed accounting of his forty-nine lifetimes on Earth.

We will, however, include his circular coded chart from page 19 of his book. Through the use of this chart and a special pendulum, combined with intensive and frequent communications with discarnate entities, Raymond Putnam Hill discovered intimate details about his past lives. These communications acquainted him with his family of souls — some forty-five entities who opened a series of incarnations originating in 5888 B.C. that continue to this day.

On September 15, 1980, Raymond Putnam Hill completed his fiftieth incarnation. Six years prior, Hill disclosed on page 141 of *My Family of Souls* that he would indeed return to 12 Wentworth Street in Charleston.

> In 2054, when I am eleven and my brother is nine, we are to take up our residence in Charleston, South Carolina. A reading about our lives there . . . predicts that we shall live in the house on Wentworth Street that I restored in 1969, and where my wife and I have since made our home. As an engineer I find no reason to doubt that this sturdy structure could be habitable a century hence; and the idea of returning to it is hardly more fantastic than being directed [there] from Hawaii [in the first place], and the incredible number of other-life associates who have found their way to us while living there.

One young Charleston couple who found their way into the life of Raymond Putnam Hill is Dr. Joseph M. "Buddy" Jenrette and his wife Betsy. Buddy came to know Mr. Hill during his 1973–1974 medical school year when he rented the bottom floor apartment, well before marrying Betsy. Warm emotions wash over Buddy's face as he recalls Raymond Hill. "He was an engaging, friendly old man with lots of energy."

Hill restored the house in 1969 when he was seventy-eight years old. Jenrette says, "Mr. Hill poured over $125,000 into the place to fix it up. People laughed at him . . . here was this old guy spending a huge sum of money and going through the headaches of fixing up an old house so late in life. What they did not realize is that he knew what he was doing. He wanted the house to be in good shape when he came back . . ."

Hill guards the house by encouraging those he likes to stay there and frightening others away. His communications are frequent, individualized, and often startling. At times he combines his affinity for high-tech wizardry with low-tech pranks.

Not long after Mr. Hill died Buddy and Betsy had the opportunity to once again live at 12 Wentworth. This time they rented the three upper floors.

For the few days they debated the move, a strange series of happenings transpired. While standing in the library, the young couple asked each other, "Should we move in?" Immediately following the question, the fluorescent lights over the bookcase turned on and a window off to their left slowly raised itself. Betsy reached over to the switch and found it in the off position. She flipped the switch — it had no effect.

The Jenrettes had seldom used these lights; the fluorescence bothered them. Plus they seemed out of place in an old nineteenth-century library. Yet twice more the lights in this room illuminated on their own accord. Both times the Jenrettes questioned their rental decision.

The idea that these initial encounters with the house might be the effects of Raymond Hill was neither foreign nor unwelcome to the Jenrettes. The couple was well acquainted with My *Family of Souls* and had discussed aspects of it with Hill when he was alive. But neither of them expected Hill to manifest as frequently and forcefully as he has in the decades since his death.

One dramatic example took place in 1981 when Betsy's friend Brad settled into the top floor dormer guestroom for a three-day visit. "He laughed at us," Buddy says. "The more we tried to tell him that there really was something to this, the more entertaining he found it. He later began laughing at Mr. Hill, taunting him by calling out around the house 'Ramie, Ramie . . . come out wherever you are' and other such nonsense."

That night after returning from dinner, the couple retired to their bedroom and Brad marched up the stairs to the top floor. Buddy remembers Brad saying goodnight as his shoes clapped the wood on the way up. Seconds later he heard Brad scream. Buddy flew up the stairs. Brad cowered on the floor against the wall pointing to his suitcase violently flapping open. Moments before, the suitcase snapped open by itself just as Brad entered the room.

Buddy helped Brad to his feet, playfully suggesting that he treat Mr. Hill with more respect.

"Yeah, right," Brad responded, rolling his eyes, trying to save face.

Then he yelled out again and crashed back to the floor. Both men watched as something dark formed against the far wall. It accumulated over a period of seconds into a concentrated mass of undulating shadow. The mass began to move with intent, forming heavily around the window near Brad's head. All at once, wind beat against the panes, the sash flew up, the mass vanished, and the window jammed wide open. Vibrations still sounded into the room as Brad scrambled his way down the stairs and out of the house.

Most encounters with Hill are not so intimidating. Yet he does seek to protect his home and his loved ones. For example, another young couple that Hill apparently liked to have in the house, Robin and Joyce Hitchcock, felt his presence constantly. When it came time for them to renew the lease, they experienced all sorts of benevolent yet bizarre phenomenon.

Suspecting that Raymond wanted them to stay, they decided to ask him directly. They sat in the den openly discussing their options, much as the Jenrettes had years earlier in the library. As they fell deeper into conversation, the thick weight of an otherworldly presence filled the room.

Robin called out, "Mr. Hill? Are you here?"

Simultaneously the mailbox buzzer rang — Hill

rigged the old house with all kinds of push button gadgetry including buttons to open curtains and one that sounded automatically upon new mail delivery — wind gassed down the chimney, and a pot of hydrangeas flew out of the fireplace.

Once when the Jenrettes visited the Hitchcocks, Betsy took a nostalgic walk with Joyce up to their old bedroom, which had also been the Hills' bedroom. The room was unbearably hot. With sweat pouring down their brows, the women went back down to tell the men about the broken air conditioning on the top floor. Moments later the two couples entered a dramatically changed room. Buddy says it was "freezing up there . . . cold as a morgue."

Yet, the discarnate Hill has no compunction about making people he dislikes absolutely miserable. One couple, whose identity will remain confidential, experienced constant difficulties operating the special electronic gadgets Mr. Hill had rigged in the house. Most annoying was the fact that the speakers snapped and popped, and CDs skipped only when they played rock music. While playing other forms of music the stereo operated flawlessly. The Jenrettes and Hitchcocks informed them that Mr. Hill's favorite music was classical and that jazz and rock annoyed him severely. Increasing frustrations with the house exacerbated a growing marital discord. The couple left the house before their lives fell completely apart. The problems between the couple resolved themselves after they moved out of 12 Wentworth.

The brunt of Hill's supernatural intimidation fell

upon the man to whom he sold the house. Chi Diep, an immigrant from a wealthy South-Vietnamese family, purchased 12 Wentworth Street in 1979. Under a special arrangement, Diep bought the house at a reduced 1979 price but Hill kept the right to live there until he died. Such an arrangement was good for Hill if he lived for a long time, good for Chi if he did not.

As it turned out, Hill developed a cancer that killed him within a year of selling the house to Chi Diep. Because he felt that he got the bad end of this deal, Hill developed an antagonism toward the new owner that lasted throughout his final year of life and beyond.

While renting from Diep, the Jenrettes witnessed Hill badgering their new landlord whenever he visited them at 12 Wentworth. The worst times occurred when Diep visited while Ruth Stone, Hill's daughter, happened to be visiting.

Chi Diep knew about Hill's animosity toward him. By this time he also knew the stories about Raymond Hill's intentional hauntings. Once, when the effusive Diep approached Ruth Stone to greet her, his glasses launched off his face and scooted across the floor. His speech quickened and his voice rose higher and higher. Finally, he shook hands with Betsy and Buddy, walked a wide circle around Ruth Stone, and quickly exited the house. Afterward Chi Diep washed his hands of Mr. Hill and his ghost. He sold the house at 12 Wentworth Street.

These stories of supernatural intimidation only portray a small part of the Raymond Putnam Hill picture. By all

Raymond Putnam Hill.

accounts, the man radiated intelligence, warmth, and compassion. An afterlife example of this occurred in 1982.

One evening the Jenrettes settled in for a quiet night alone together. While the fire popped and hissed, they read on the couch with blankets pulled over their legs. Throughout the old house, all was tranquil.

Suddenly, the mailbox buzzer rang wildly. It rang with such annoying persistence that Buddy ran to look out the window. At the mailbox all was still. No one was there. Buddy looked both ways down the street and checked the mailbox. He saw nothing and the mailbox was empty.

Five minutes later the buzzer rang again with greater urgency. This time the Jenrettes walked out of the house to find their friend Franz Thur on the street, bruised, bleeding, and semi-conscious.

That evening Franz nearly killed himself by consuming too much alcohol and forgetting to take his diabetes medication. In the years before Mr. Hill died, Franz rented the same apartment on the bottom floor that Buddy had in 1973. He missed Mr. Hill and often came by the house to reminisce with the Jenrettes about the big souled old man.

Franz died a few years after this incident. But had the strange clanging buzzer not startled the Jenrettes into searching the street, Franz would have died in the gutter that night rather than later in peaceful dignity.

As Buddy Jenrette puts it, "Mr. Hill was signaling that Franz was out there and needed help. Franz saw no one. There is no other explanation."

◆

New stories about Mr. Hill's activities will no doubt continue to surface. But the most satisfying will be the one told in 2054, when after a long strange journey, an eleven-year-old boy and his nine-year-old brother move into the house at 12 Wentworth Street, and feel thoroughly at home.

THE GENTLEMAN GHOST

In 1904 an unhappy young man returned from Yale University to the family estate at 20 South Battery, a towering, five-story mansion with a mansard roof. He ascended the stairs to the top floor and "fell" from the window onto the lawn below. This story is undeniably tragic. However, the ghost story connected with it is not.

The Gentleman Ghost consistently reappears in room 10 of the Battery Carriage House Inn. Persons fortunate enough to meet him describe a wispy gray apparition, a handsome young man of medium height with a slight build and a receding hairline. His clothing places him from the heart of Charleston's Victorian period. The Gentleman Ghost proceeds through the afterlife undaunted, demonstrating an obvious affinity for women. Perhaps he is making up for what he missed by dying so young.

Those who encounter this apparition praise his demeanor and manners. He is a genteel ghost who does not act threatening in any way. However, most of his appearances seem to be motivated by his desire to jump into bed with women staying in room 10.

When the ghostly young man appears lying beside her, a woman's usual response is to scream. That is when the Gentleman Ghost politely exits through the wall.

Such behavior suggests that he chooses to leave rather than impose himself on a lady, as this would be unbecoming for a man of his refined sensibilities and social stature. This is how the Gentleman Ghost acquired both his reputation and his name.

The following is a letter to the proprietor, Drayton Hastie, from a former Inn guest who wishes to remain anonymous. In it, she describes the spectral visit she experienced in 1992:

> In celebration of our birthday, my twin sister and I decided to treat ourselves to an overnight stay at the well-known Carriage House Inn on the Battery in Charleston, South Carolina. The date was May 19, 1992. The room was furnished in the lovely antique-style furnishings of the 1800s. My sister and I both love historic places, so we were pleased with the atmosphere of the historic Carriage House. We were given room 10. Our common wall was connected to the main house.
>
> We retired for the night about 11 P.M. I placed one of the antique chairs in front of the door, telling my sister that if anyone tried to enter, the chair would be a barrier. My sister fell asleep almost immediately. I was restless and couldn't fall asleep. I was lying on the right side of the bed, facing the door. I noticed a wispy, gray apparition that appeared to be floating through the closed door, through the chair, and into the room.

The configuration was of a man with no visible features. His height was about 5 feet 8 inches. No special clothes were visible, just a gray, wispy shape of a slightly built man. He moved in an upright gliding motion over to my side of the bed. He lay down in a twelve-inch space beside me on the bed. He placed his right arm around my shoulders. I didn't feel any pressure from his arm touching me. At no time did he speak to me. I wasn't frightened because he didn't seem threatening.

I wanted to wake my sister to let her see what was happening. I called her name several times before she woke up. She asked me what was wrong. When I tried to answer her, the figure disappeared more suddenly than he had appeared. I didn't say anything else to her, but relaxed and fell asleep and didn't awake until 6 A.M. I then asked my sister if she had seen or heard anything in the night. She hadn't. I related my story of the visitor during the night. She was disappointed she hadn't seen him herself.

I wished I had remained quiet and not spoken, because I feel I frightened him away. I feel that possibly the restoration and renovation of the main house were disturbing his home. He was looking for a place to rest and thought we might share our bed for the night.

I would love to return some day and spend another night at the Carriage House Inn to see if my Gentleman Visitor revisits me.

What happens when the woman remains quiet? To date, we have no reports of that.

THE HEADLESS TORSO

Most Charleston ghosts comport themselves with the refined behavior and appearance of the people and of the city. However, the specter occupying room 8 at the Battery Carriage House Inn, located behind the mansion at 20 South Battery, is as menacing as he is ugly. His countenance is atypically brutal.

What makes this ghost so awful is that he has no head. Visitors report seeing the torso of a man clad in a coarse wool outer garment. This ghost marks his appearances with a guttural moan as though he is in deep pain. At times, he hovers at arm's length. More often, he parades in erect military posture back and forth at the foot of the bed.

Although some maintain that he is the remnant of a pirate hanged in the oaks at Battery Park, the preponderance of experience suggests he is the ghost of a Confederate soldier who lost his head and the greater part of his limbs during a munitions explosion accident.

Across the street from the mansion, White Point

Gardens now covers the once dug out fort and Confederate munitions magazine known as Battery Ramsey. In February 1865, Charleston residents evacuated the city, many taking family and valuables to the capital in Columbia, 120 miles inland, to avoid the wrath and ravage of General William Tecumseh Sherman's great March to the Sea. In fact Sherman spared Charleston and obliterated Columbia, where so many Charlestonians sought refuge, and where he left little trace of flourishing antebellum life.

To this day, mystery surrounds Sherman's decision not to unleash the full hell of his army onto Charleston as a real and symbolic act of revenge toward the city that started the murderous Civil War. In his public role as warrior, Sherman's regard for Charleston was clearly negative. He bastardized the city's proper name with terms such as "the hellhole of secession."

The answer to this mystery may lie within the man's private world where his regard for Charleston held deep paradox. Earlier in his career, Sherman served at Fort Moultrie on Sullivan's Island. During this period (1842–1845) the city sparkled with wealth and vitality in spite of the stock market crash of 1841. Then as now, Charleston stood alone among America's cities as an elite visual jewel.

Across harbor water from the fort, the dazzling city shimmered in the young Sherman's sights each night. He enjoyed Charleston's social life and developed friendships with local families. Did the young soldier have a lover in the city? Or did the city itself create a soft place in his heart?

After the evacuation of Charleston, Confederates exploded tons of their own munitions along the waterfront at the tip of the peninsula. They worked fast and furiously to do whatever it took to keep the weaponry out of enemy hands, believing that Sherman's approach to the city was imminent. One prominent artillery piece, a giant Blakely gun from England, sat at what is now the corner of South Battery and East Bay Streets. Upon exploding, a huge fragment of the gun flew into the roof of the Thomas Roper House at 9 East Battery and lodged into the rafters, where it remains today.

Five houses away at 20 South Battery, the soldiers in charge of destroying the remaining munitions took nightly refuge in the carriage house behind the deserted mansion. This dangerous work — great blasts performed in haste — may explain the horrible wounds inflicted on the body of what now exists as a floating, headless torso in room 8. The poor soul who sought rest there during his final days of duty returns a disturbed and restless disfigured aura in the afterlife.

On the night of Saturday, August 8, 1992, the Headless Torso visited a couple in room 8. Eight months later in a taped testimony recorded at the law office of Drayton Hastie, proprietor of the Battery Carriage House Inn, the couple revealed the details of their encounter with this angry apparition.

Hastie Interview, July 10, 1993:

HUSBAND: I am a skeptic. I'm a technical person by education, an engineer. I believe in things I can see and feel and so on and I have never been a believer in things supernatural, or ghosts, or spirits, [until] last August 8. We came to Charleston and got a room at the Battery Carriage House Inn for the evening.

Like I said, I have never been a believer in anything like this. In fact, after it happened, I still for a while thought it was just a dream . . . but the more I thought about it, the more I realized that it wasn't just a dream, because it was too real.

The bed in that room is sort of an antique bed that sits higher off the floor than a bed you would have today. So when you lie down on it you are not at [the usual] level, but up a little higher. I slept on the right hand side and [my wife] slept on the left side . . . I was sleeping on my side facing away from the bed looking at the wall . . . I don't know what time it was. I don't remember. It wasn't early in the morning and it wasn't right after I fell asleep.

It was sometime in the middle of the night that I had a sensation of being watched. What I could see laying on my side with my head on the pillow was this torso of a person from the waist to the neck. I couldn't see a face. I couldn't see legs or feet but I could see its body.

It was a man. It was big, not necessarily tall but broad. A strong, barrel-chested man. He had on several layers of clothing. His overcoat was, and I distinctly remember this because I reached out and touched it . . . his overcoat was of very coarse material like burlap — it was very scratchy.

Looking back on it, touching this thing is one of the two things that make me think it was more than just a dream. I had the real physical sensation of touching something. I remember that clearly, it wasn't just seeing it in a dream. It was a real feeling of touching.

The other thing was that this person breathed, and it was sort of raspy, like he had asthma or allergies or something. But when I reached out and touched his coat, the breath changed into the guttural growl of an animal.

He moaned, or uttered some angry sound that made it clear that he didn't want me to do what I was doing. It was threatening. This thing didn't have an axe or a knife to kill me, but he was not happy that I was there. I felt like he wanted to chase me out of there.

It really scared the heck out of me. It really did. Again, I am not a believer of things like this.

INTERVIEWER: Why would you want to reach out?

HUSBAND: I think because the material looked so unusual to me. It was not like any overcoat I had ever seen before. I was curious. It looked so different that I had to reach out and touch it. It was open. I don't remember seeing buttons or clasps or anything. It was just open like a cape or an overcoat, just draped over the shoulders. It was very thick. You could see the fibers like you can with a burlap sack. Fibers stuck right out of it.

WIFE: You said you felt danger.

HUSBAND: Yes, after I touched his coat, I felt fear. I was very much afraid. I felt that at any moment he was going to harm me . . . I know everyone has had a dream where you try to scream and you can't. And that is what I tried to do, to scream. I was that frightened. He was standing, then hovering right over me. There was that much room between the bed and the wall. He was standing in the space between the bed and the wall, right next to me. I didn't even have to stretch to touch him . . . he was a foot or a foot and a half away.

WIFE: You got a gut feeling that it was a real person or an intruder or a burglar?

HUSBAND: I never saw hands, I never saw a neck, I never saw legs, I just saw a torso. But it was a person. It wasn't just a coat. There was a real person there, yet there was no — like I said, I never saw a face, I never saw flesh.

INTERVIEWER: But you are sure it was a man?

HUSBAND: Yes, I am positive it was a man from the depth of his breathing. It was a very low, deep wheezing. It is still hard for me to believe. But what I know is that it was more than just a dream . . . it was real and physical. I am still not going to sit here and say it was a spirit, but I can't think of what else it was.

INTERVIEWER: What was his hair like?

HUSBAND: I couldn't see any. There was a person there. There was noise. The things that scared me the most and convinced me it wasn't a dream was what I heard and what I felt.

INTERVIEWER: So, what made you come back here?

HUSBAND: Well ever since it happened I cannot stop talking about it. I told one person and then another and another. I haven't gone around broadcasting it because it can feel ridiculous telling people about it. But I can't stop. I can't seem to help it.

[My wife] kept telling me, "You've got to call the owner of the house and find out the history. You need to find out if something happened there and if there are other people who have this experience."

The more I thought about it, the more I thought she was right. I needed to dig back, ask questions, and *find out* . . . It's like I am now the one with unfinished business.

WIFE: There is so much history here, it makes sense that if indeed there are such things as ghosts they would exist in these old homes.

CLOSING COMMENTS BY MR. HASTIE: I want to put on tape that [the husband] was trained as an industrial engineer. He is not a believer in any supernatural events or, as he says, at least he wasn't before now.

No mention was made to him or to his wife of the experience of the sisters from California [who were delighted with their visit from the Gentleman Ghost] or of prior supernatural events transpiring in room 8 or room 10. The strange thing is that from all accounts it appears that there are two different people who are conducting the visits to these rooms.

[The husband's] visitor was clearly not the young man. I think I will continue to hold to the awake/dream theory . . . I think that when you are in a strange place away from home, it is more normal to have dreams of apprehension. At any rate, we will keep collecting our ghost stories and see if the consistency of the stories continue to match.

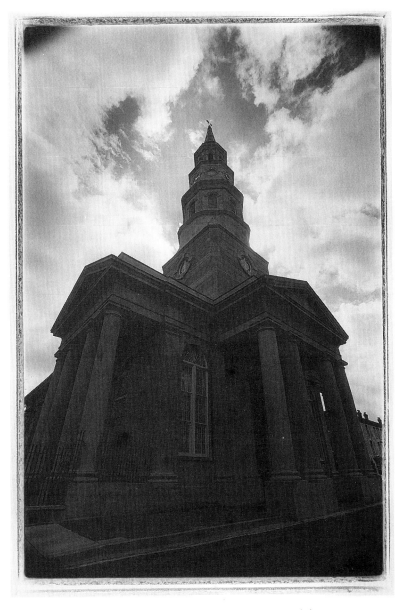

St. Philip's Church. A silent player in many of the stories.

Staircase to the Past

On the southeastern corner of St. Michael's Alley, overlooking the church's cemetery, stands the white single house 76 Meeting Street. The Republican Judge Elihu Bay purchased the house circa 1784. By the time his decades of service to Charleston law ended, two ghosts forever attached themselves to his name: one a young man he tried to help, the other a beautiful woman named Lavinia Fisher whom he sentenced to be hanged in 1819 — the first woman to be hanged in South Carolina. Her story is recounted in literature about Charleston legends.

One night in 1812 Judge Bay awoke to the sounds of obnoxiously inebriated young men bounding down St. Michael's Alley and onto his piazza. His son, carried up the stairs by friends, bellowed the loudest of them all. For days afterwards Judge Bay gave one terse reply to neighbors inquiring about his son and the happenings of that night. Shaking his big head, disgust written all over his face, he muttered, "Drunk, drunk, and a Democrat," and abruptly marched on.

Judge Bay's contempt for his son's wastrel ways stemmed from similar events that took place twenty-six years earlier. One August night in 1786 another set of young men advanced through St. Michael's Alley. No one knows why that fun evening turned so dark, why young men with so much life yet to live turned to pistols to settle a drunken argument. Surely, filled with whiskey, they did not fully understand either.

Judge Bay heard the yelling just outside his windows. Pistol shots rang out. He flung open his door in time to see young men carrying a body splayed out in a bloody mess. They took the man, blood pumping onto the banister and stairs, up the staircase into the front bedroom on the second floor. Upon leaving him on his deathbed, the young men fled into the muggy night. The man died in that room before the doctor arrived.

Soon after the duelist's death, his ghost found itself trapped in 76 Meeting Street, doomed to the hell of repeating a wasted life's final moments. Near midnight on otherwise still, quiet nights, residents of this house hear boots scrambling onto the piazza and up the staircase. Mingled into and sometimes completely drowning out the scrambling flurry of footsteps is the awful sound of a limp body being dragged up the stairs. The feet strike each step of the staircase. When the ghostly group reaches the top of the stairs, the heaved body can be heard falling onto the bed in the room where the duelist actually died.

This supernatural event is unique because not only is the ghost of the slain man heard, but also the ghosts of his six companions. From the guilt of having left their friend to die, their ghosts have been condemned to noisily tread that staircase into eternity; an echo from the past.

◆

In 1942, St. Michael's Church converted the house into its rectory. That silenced the ghost; no reports of his haunting exist after 1942. One theory for this happening is that specters cannot exist under the same roof with the Episcopal cloth. Another is that the presence of priests healed the Duelist Ghost, liberating him from the torture of forever repeating his final moments.

The Sword Gates House

The high brick walls encasing the fine gardens of 32 Legare Street were not always so high. André Talvande and his wife Ann built these around the grounds of the fine antebellum school for girls that they ran. They stand a reminder of the scandalous elopement of one of their wealthiest students, Maria Whaley.

Maria Whaley lived most of her charmed young life on Pine Baron Plantation, the main Whaley family holding on Edisto Island. The family had no plans to send Maria away to school. Yet, when a handsome young man named George Morris began to call more and more frequently on their fifteen-year-old daughter, they scrambled to get Maria out of his sights.

By this time, the Whaleys had become accustomed to Maria attracting the attention of young men. However, with George Morris came two unsettling factors the Whaleys had not dealt with before. The first was that Maria's eyes transformed in the presence of Morris. Maria knew she was attractive. She also knew that her eyes, more than most people's, were windows to her soul. She was quiet, but not shy.

At first glance, the girl looked virginal, wide-eyed,

and innocent. Maria's eyes held the wonder of untouched magical worlds — layers upon layers of them. Normally, she hid them from full view, glancing to the side and down, holding back from showing more. She knew their power and treated them as a gift to be protected, not as a weapon to be used for personal power.

But when she did look at someone straight on, the reaction was never casual. Those wide, virginal eyes invited wildness and excitement. Doors unlocked and opened, one after another, unfolding deeper into unending caverns of wonder. Men got lost there. Women lost themselves in envy.

Maria's effect on men was nothing new to the Whaleys. What disturbed them was George's effect on Maria. Whenever George entered their home, Maria's eyes beamed rays of joy.

For the Whaleys, the second unsettling factor about George Morris concerned the fact that he was a New Yorker. Most people hearing this story today believe that this fact of George's origins was their sole problem with him as a potential husband for Maria. Yet, tensions between North and South at this time, 1828, had not advanced to the fiery degree of the decades to come. The fact was that in 1828, Charleston had in its midst an abundance of the most wealthy families in America. George Morris, though not poor by any means, had not the vast fortunes of the Charleston Rice Lord families and the Whaleys desired for Maria to marry "one of her own kind."

To discourage the romance, Mr. Whaley forbid George to call on Maria at the house. To prove his resolve to Maria and to the community at large, he spent an entire day on his horse galloping around Edisto Island persuading all neighbors to refuse George Morris lodging. Colonel Whaley returned home satisfied with himself and the thoroughness of his actions.

But the very next evening, a Black man came to the door of his great house. "Colonel Whaley suh, dat man Morris dun putch a tent on de west side of de island, roastin' a big fat pig."

Exasperated, Colonel Whaley marched up the stairs to Maria's room and commanded her to pack her clothes, to get ready for school.

"But father, I do not have school until Monday morning."

"Get ready. You are going to a different school."

That weekend the Colonel and his wife drove Maria in their horse-drawn coach to Legare Street. It was there, in what is now called the Sword Gates House, that Madame Talvande and her husband ran a school for girls. The Whaleys believed that under their strong, watchful eye, Maria would not only be shielded from Morris, but also experience directly the charms of the world they wanted their daughter to marry into.

Once again Morris foiled their plans. He found Maria and soon after, planned to elope and marry at St. Michael's Church. The elopement was an affair right out of one of Maria's magical hidden worlds. Cold rain fell at night during a late winter storm. Candlelight flickered all around the altar of St. Michael's and extended down the empty aisles.

"SWORD GATES" HOUSE

C·1808

WOODEN PORTION OF BUILDING WHICH HOUSED NOTED SCHOOL OF MADAME TALVANDE WAS EN- LARGED BY MASONRY ADDITION IN 1849 BY GEORGE HOPLEY. BRITISH CONSUL. HE BUILT THE WALL AND INSTALLED THE FAMOUS GATES MADE BY THE OUTSTANDING CHRISTOPHER WERNER. ADGERS. SIMONTONS.ALSTONS AND A DE- SCENDANT OF ABRAHAM LINCOLN ARE AMONG THE PROMINENT FAMILIES WHO HAVE OWNED THIS HANDSOME PROPERTY.

PLACED BY
THE PRESERVATION SOCIETY OF CHARLESTON

George waited with the minister and a few friends. All plans hinged upon Maria's successful escape from Madame Talvande's house and scaling the walls in a wide hoop-skirted wedding dress.

When the front door to the church opened, relief

swept through George. Maria's eyes shot sparkles. Joy radiated through everyone in St. Michael's that night, and love enveloped the couple with the warm certainty of its own laws of righteousness.

Maria did not sleep with George that night. Nor did the couple immediately leave town. Secrecy was important for the wedding ceremony only. Afterwards, the couple desired to depart in an elaborate demonstration of chivalrous style, befitting to a woman of Maria's social standing. Maria returned to school that night, just blocks away from the church, and gathered her belongings, waiting for George's return the next day.

He returned, dashing, dressed in fine clothes, and riding up in a resplendent coach. All the schoolgirls gathered at the windows, pushing and shoving for the best view of this mysterious, handsome gentleman advancing up the walk to the school's front door.

"I am here for Mrs. Morris," he declared to the housekeeper.

Madame Talvande overheard the request and, perplexed, came to the door. "Except for myself, there are no married women here. There is no Mrs. Morris here. This is a school for girls. Who are you young man?"

"I am George Morris, and I am here to pick up my wife."

Commotion stirred in adjoining rooms as the excited girls shrieked and laughed. "Quiet girls!" Madame Talvande barked over her shoulder. "Just one minute Mr. Morris." She shut the door.

Madame Talvande snapped an order at her students

to behave and marched them outside onto the lawn. When they were all calmed and in line, she wryly called out, "Girls, this is Mr. Morris who says he is here to pick up his wife. Is there a Mrs. Morris present among us?"

No one said a word for seconds. The girls looked up and down the row at each other. Then Maria stepped forward, at first tentatively, then she looked up at George, smiling broadly, eyes beaming, and said, "Yes, I am."

The shock first rendered Madame Talvande speechless. Then the stiff schoolmistress lost all composure, screaming at Maria and then at members of her staff. George whisked Maria into the long black coach and the powerful steeds hoofed the couple out of sight.

Maria and George took their gallant risk and reaped the rewards of a life together forged from an inner knowing in a time when pressure to follow the rules was far greater than it is today. From what we know about the lives of George and Maria, they truly did live happily ever after.

However, the scandal rocked the Charleston social scene and deeply unsettled Madame Talvande and the members of her staff. The elite school was built on trust, and although Charlestonians and the Whaleys soon forgave the schoolmistress as well as the young lovers, Madame Talvande still believed she should have prevented the elopement. This was the time of slavery, a time when rich Charlestonians could fool themselves and pull off the notion of forever being able to control other human beings.

Madame Talvande carried guilt over the episode. Her eyes constantly watch the old house. Her ghost reveals itself in two places. The first is the top floor piazza where she stands peering over the lush grounds of the Sword Gates House. Her eyes flicker bright orange with great focus and intensity. The rest of her manifests in colors of blue and gold.

She also haunts the stateroom on the top floor, the room where the schoolgirls once slept. The knob will turn and the door pop open. Oftentimes all that comes through the open door is a cool breeze. But during major hauntings, Madame Talvande appears in full dress, eyes on fire, crossing slowly from one end of the room to the other. She hovers far off the wood floor, surveying the stateroom, guarding her flock, and her reputation, from anyone attempting to intrude or escape.

Elizabeth and Zoe Saint Amand

The Queen Street Shadow

On a busy Friday night in the summer of 1995, the French Quarter restaurant Poogan's Porch at 72 Queen Street hosted one of the many spectral returns of Zoe Saint Amand. What makes her returns distinctive is that nothing marks her appearance as otherworldly. She walks through the restaurant, an elderly lady dressed in a long black dress, offering no clues that she is a ghost.

A twenty-two-year-old student named Maria Cartillo worked the hostess stand that evening. Shortly after midnight the last of dinner guests exited into the steamy night. Maria sighed with relief and began to assist the staff with the two hour process of closing down the restaurant.

She heard the door to the restaurant swing open behind her. All night, whenever guests had opened the door, humid air from outside had rushed in to replace the cool air in the foyer. But this time when the door opened, the incoming air was cold. The hallway was empty when Maria looked over her shoulder. She advanced carefully toward the entrance, bewildered by the wide-open door and the sudden cold.

As she closed the door, she looked at the panes of

the window to her left. The bottom panes, usually wet from the confluence of air conditioning and humidity, were covered with frost. She looked higher up in the window and screamed. The reflection showed an old woman in a black dress standing right behind her.

Maria quickly regained her composure and offered her greetings. The old woman silently turned from her, walked down the hall past the hostess stand, and entered the back dining room.

Maria thought about how upset the staff would be with her for seating a new guest after closing time. Nevertheless, she was determined to be gracious to the late arrival. Entering the dining room, Maria saw that the old lady in the black dress had seated herself. She sat looking down at her folded hands.

Maria approached her. "Your server will be with you soon," she said. "Would you like to order something to drink?"

The old woman slowly raised her head and smiled grimly, before vanishing from her seat.

Zoe Saint Amand was born in Charleston in 1879. Her father, Emile Saint Amand, made his living as a traveling salesman and was seldom home. Her mother, also named Zoe, died when Zoe was only six years old. At that early age Zoe began what turned out to be a life distinguished by solitude.

Elizabeth (Liz) Saint Amand, her older sister by two years, became Zoe's one close lifetime companion. After their father died in 1907, the girls continued to live

Mrs. Deery with Bon Ami.

together. Over the course of sixty-six years, they lived together in various homes around the city. They last lived together in the house at 72 Queen Street.

Both women were teachers. Liz taught art and spent time with her bohemian set of friends. Zoe taught grade school at the Crafts School on the corner of Legare and Queen Streets, but did not make much time in her life for friends. Teaching was her life.

Neither of the sisters married. By the 1930s, Zoe epitomized the stereotypical spinster. She appeared puritanical, wearing round, wire-rimmed glasses, black dresses with high necks, with her hair styled into a tight bun. Her stern clothes and the effect of her isolated existence made Zoe look decades older than her real age.

Mr. and Mrs. Deery also lived at 72 Queen in the 1930s. The sisters rented the downstairs; the Deerys had the top floor. According to Mr. Deery and students of Zoe's who still live around Charleston, Zoe Saint Amand was regarded as brilliant, but eccentric, her whole life. For some reason she chose to speak with an English accent.

Zoe had one best friend other than Liz; a black and white cat named Bon Ami, who lived to be 23 years old and died in the early 1940s.

In 1945, Elizabeth became ill and passed away. Without her cat, her sister, or her teaching profession, Zoe became lost. She went from being a quiet and eccentric spinster to virtually disappearing from the radar of humanity. In such extreme isolation, her mental health deteriorated quickly.

Although rarely seen, Zoe lived nine years after her sister's death. She continued to live alone at 72 Queen Street. From time to time, she was seen in the upstairs windows, alternately calling out her sister's name and beckoning people on the sidewalk to come in to visit. Finally family friends took her to live her last two years at the old St. Francis Hospital. She spent her remaining time there, as did many elderly Catholic Charleston widows and spinsters without family.

Zoe Saint Amand died quietly in the winter of 1954. Her body rests at St. Lawrence Cemetery on the neck of the Charleston peninsula, next to her beloved sister Elizabeth, and near the graves of the parents she hardly knew. Her death was barely noticed by anyone, including the Crafts School where she had given so much of her life energy for nearly fifty years.

On an inclement winter night in 1997, six elderly women took The Ghosts of Charleston walking tour. As cold drizzle glistened in the arc of the streetlights, the group took shelter inside Poogan's Porch. Before the guide began his story, one of the ladies pointed a bony finger at a photograph on the wall. It was a 1940s black and white print, hanging crooked in a minimal black frame. From that picture stared the faces of two women, looking as elderly in the 1940s photograph as this group on tour was in 1997.

One of the women in the picture wore a comfortable looking light colored dress, the other a stern black corset and shawl. The lady pointing at the picture declared in a strong Charleston accent, tinged with a tone of awe, "My God, there's Zoe Cinnamon!"

The guide corrected her, "No ma'am that's Zoe Saint Amand."

As the rest of the group listened with polite earnestness, the one who recognized the face shot back, "No, young man. Zoe Cinnamon is what we called her when she taught us grade school down at the Crafts School on Legare in the early Twenties."

Amazed, the guide begged her for more information. "Do you remember anything about her?"

"Yes, she was very stern. She made us cut the erasers off all of our pencils on the first day of school. She said it was to keep us from being tempted to make mistakes."

The house at 72 Queen Street, which she and her sister rented for nearly thirty years, became a restaurant called Poogan's Porch in 1976. It was then that Zoe returned.

Sometimes late at night, guests looking out from their rooms on the Queen Street side of the Mills House Hotel will glimpse an old woman in a black dress mechanically waving from the second floor window of the restaurant. Her face is sad and utterly devoid of animation.

Often their first reaction is alarm, believing an elderly patron of Poogan's has been locked inside. They phone the police or hotel management. When the police ascend the staircase to the second floor, their flashlights playing along the walls, they find that whomever or whatever beckoned from the second floor window gone — or at least hidden from plain sight.

Charles Ball, father-in-law of restaurant owner Bobbie Ball, knows from firsthand experience that Zoe is not gone when she cannot be seen. During the holiday season in 1991, Charles brought a cup of coffee and carpentry tools into the restaurant well after 2 A.M. The middle of the night was the only time he could make repairs without disturbing the restaurant's guests. He placed his tools near the main floor stairway and began to repair a loose bannister.

Suddenly, pots and pans crashed in the kitchen, a tremendous clatter that lasted for over fifteen seconds. Charles thought that part of the roof had come down. When the crashing stopped, he ran to inspect the damage. Inside the kitchen, everything remained arranged in perfect order. He opened cupboards and drawers only to discover a disturbing normalcy. The terrible noise, still ringing in his ears, had no apparent source.

Stunned and shaking in disbelief, Charles stumbled back to the stairway where he had been working and grabbed his cup of coffee. His cup was empty. On the rim was a pale stain of lipstick.

Charles Ball put the cup down, grabbed his toolbox, and ran out to his truck on Queen Street. He would finish his work later — in the presence of humanity.

The one defining aspect of the ghost of Zoe Saint Amand is that it craves attention. This spirit seems to exist in order to interact with humanity. She longs to escape from her universe of lonely wandering. The sad irony is that her desire to connect with living people now that she is dead is exactly what seals her trap in a lost dimension.

The Lady in White

In the fall of 1906, Edward Whitridge of Mount Pleasant became ill. He lived with Mary, his wife of thirty years, in the small town just a short ferry ride east of Charleston across the Cooper River. The sickness came on so gradually that he did not notice its severity until one day he could scarcely breathe. Just making his way up the stairs to his bedroom became a dreaded ordeal. Lying in bed in the middle of the night, he often hacked so loudly that his startled wife jolted upright.

Edward rolled his own blend of South Carolina tobacco. Lighting a cigarette was his first action every morning; he stamped one out before closing his eyes each night. Mary pleaded with him to stop. The doctors also suggested he quit, but they lacked the diagnostic technology to know the cause of his illness with scientific certainty. The best diagnosis they offered him was that he was a general "consumptive." They advised him to stop smoking, but only if he felt it might be interfering with his recovery from the mysterious "consumption."

At the time, Mary was sixty-one years old and not in good health herself. She could breathe normally but oftentimes felt light-headed even after the mildest exercise. She lamented her husband's decline because their marriage of over thirty years had been a joyous one. She also feared it; she did not want to live her remaining years alone and without his physical assistance. She alternated the tactics of her assaults on his smoking between harsh nagging and soft appeal. Whenever Mary brought it up, Edward defensively recounted the doctors' hedged advice. Then he would add, "My father lived into his eighties, and he smoked all his life." He loved his wife, had no desire to die, and did not consider his smoking to be the cause of his illness, so he kept smoking.

Soon Edward became so sick that he strained for each breath. In a desperate attempt to find a cure to the mysterious "consumption," Mary convinced him to go to Baltimore. She hoped that the renowned physicians at Johns Hopkins would find a cure for his illness.

Edward boarded a ship leaving from Charleston Harbor on the evening of January 11, 1907. He never made it to Baltimore. He died en route — two days later — not of asphyxiation, but of a heart attack. In the autopsy, the doctors in Baltimore revealed a gummed and bloated heart, tired from all those years of tar and nicotine exposure.

An even sadder fact about Edward's death is that no one came to claim his remains. Officials from the Baltimore morgue sent a letter to Mary, but received no response. They kept his body for thirty days, then buried him at the expense of Baltimore's taxpayers.

Mary never received the letter. On January 13, on her way up the stairs to the bedroom, Mary's breathing became strained. Before she made it into bed, she clutched her chest and collapsed. She and her husband died of heart failure on the same day.

Mary Whitridge's body lies in the iron-gated Whitridge family plot in the center of the Unitarian Church Graveyard in Charleston. Next to her is an empty space where her husband's grave should be. During life, Mary and Edward enjoyed taking strolls after church through the Unitarian's lush foliage that cascades over headstones and brick walk-ways. Because of Fate's unfortunate timing, husband and wife reside far apart from each other in death.

The ghost of Mary Whitridge radiates a brilliant white aura. She hovers effortlessly over the dense foliage that surrounds the Unitarian Church. However, a sharp feeling of tension accompanies her bright manifestations in the graveyard. The pure whiteness of her spirit is a beautiful thing to behold. At the same time, she permeates the area around her with a lost, wandering sadness.

Many mediums or "sensitives" as they sometimes prefer to be called, venture into this florid graveyard with us on The Ghosts of Charleston tour. They attribute this haunting to the power of love to exist beyond the grave. Mary Whitridge exists in her own world of sad searching, looking for her lost soul mate. Unfortunately, the action that might allow her to rest, her husband's exhumation and relocation from Baltimore to the Unitarian Graveyard in Charleston, is unlikely.

She also exists to protect or warn those who are in danger of dying as her husband did. Dan Petterson of Petterson Antiques on the corner of King and Fulton Streets feels grateful to the Lady in White. In the following interview, he described an event that occurred in September 1985 at 10:30 P.M. that proved to be life changing:

DP (DAN PETTERSON): I was walking back home from my store late one night after doing inventory work. As I usually did,

I cut through the Unitarian Graveyard. It is not only scenic, but also a quick shortcut back to my apartment.

I was right in the dense area near the border of the Lutheran Graveyard, where the foliage is very thick and weedy. I had my Zippo lighter out and was just getting ready to light up a cigarette. It was then that I saw the ghost.

EM (Ed Macy): What did it look like?

DP: She was aglow with a whitish light from her head down to the feet. But the thing that made me stare was the way she was moving. . . .

EM: How was that?

DP: She was undulating, moving side to side very slowly, in waves.

EM: What happened next?

DP: It looked so strange and intriguing that I started walking towards the apparition. The closer I got to it, the more it began to fade in to the extreme darkness of the churchyard. . . . By the time I got to where it had been, it was completely gone. It just vanished into thin air.

I then realized I was standing, almost literally, on a gravestone. On a whim I can't explain, I flicked the lighter to read the stone. The grave I was standing on belonged to a man named Edward Ferry. I knew him! We were acquaintances in school, over at St. Andrew's High School, years ago. I knew he had passed . . . smoking in bed. He died in the fire. I didn't know he was buried right behind my store!

EM: What did you do next?

DP: I crumpled the cigarette in my pocket. I never lit it. I never smoked another cigarette again to this day, almost fourteen years later. I think the Lady in White was trying to tell me something. She wanted to show me his grave for a reason... I've always considered her a sort of a guardian angel. She may well have saved me from death by smoking.

"Yesterday for me & today for thee," reads the inscription on the headstone of mariner Thomas Poole in St. Philip's Graveyard.

The Haunt of the Dock Street Theatre

In the fall of 1839, a young woman with big dark eyes and a striking figure entered the first floor of Charleston's bawdy Planters Hotel alone. Neither the girl nor the establishment would ever be the same.

Cigar smoke saturated the saloon atmosphere. Noise permeated the place with physical force. Whiskey and money flowed. Singers accompanied energetic piano playing, and well-dressed but inebriated card players belted out loud commands and laughter.

The crowd hushed at the sight of her. She wore an elegant red dress with her hair pulled up off her delicate shoulders and arranged in a sophisticated manner on the top of her head. She stood still, poised on the outside, nervous and shaking on the inside. Not knowing what to do next, she held in this manner, unmoving, and waited for events to turn her way.

One year before, twenty-five-year-old Nettie Dickerson had arrived in Charleston from far inland and began work in the parish offices of the South's most prestigious Episcopal Church — St. Philip's on Church Street. Her small town priest arranged for her to make her start in Charleston there.

Because she exuded charm and a country girl reverence for the Charleston elite, parishioners at St. Philip's found her personality refreshing. The priests found her useful in running errands, delivering messages in person to Charleston gentry, and organizing elegant social events. In return, Nettie received room and board a few blocks from the church, a small clothing allowance, and the opportunity to meet the people who ruled Charleston society.

Well before she turned twenty-five years old, Nettie had exhausted the possibilities of eligible bachelors in her sparsely populated upcountry county. There had been some decent prospects — but Nettie could not endure the thought of committing to a life of social boredom in the country. Charleston constantly drove her imagination until in 1838, she found her way there.

Unfortunately for Nettie, as cosmopolitan as the city was, Charleston did not prove to be the land of opportunity she dreamed it would be. Slave labor took most of the service work in which she excelled, and rich men looking for wives did not search for prospects among working women. Pretty as she was, in a time when seventeen was the prime marrying age for women, twenty-five-year-old Nettie was considered a spinster. Antebellum Charleston, a place of riches and opportunity for many, proved not to be the land of plenty for a woman of Nettie's ilk.

Because of her good looks, many rich men approached her, desiring her as a mistress. Eventually, Nettie took advantage of their attentions as a vehicle to explore Charleston's highlife. But before long, the ambitious Nettie began to resent the freedom and hypocrisy of the men in the world around her. On Sundays, pious looking planters and merchants paraded their dignified wives and perfectly attired children down the aisles for worship in the many houses of God along Church Street. Many of these same men spent weekday nights directly across the street whoring and drinking at the Planters Hotel.

She also grew to resent her boring work life and the reality that she was without money. Nettie longed to escape the tensions festering both inside her and on the street that so narrowly divided saint from sinner. One day, she climbed the stairs to the St. Philip's bell tower. High above the noise of commerce, Nettie's imagination soared with the breeze that blew through her hair. Up there her dreams of living like one of the Charleston aristocracy seemed possible.

Looking down from the steeple height, all people appeared the same to her. She reflected on the strange values of a city where a high-class whorehouse luridly flaunted its trade across the street from elite places of worship. Some of the owners of the nationally renowned Planters Hotel attended holy services across the street, and contributed substantially to church coffers. It puzzled her why society regarded these people as better than she was.

Many afternoons, Nettie encased herself in the safety of the steeple. From on high she watched the frequent electrical storms rapidly thunder out to sea. Below, people scrambled for cover. Nettie laughed and let the wind wash her with rainwater. Often chilled, but always invigorated, she stared in silent rapture as the fierce bolts forked through the dark skies.

Walking along Church Street one evening, lightning cracked not far from her. Something drew her to look back at the church. She stopped, fascinated by the great bronze cross shining at the pinnacle of the spire, and at the ornate lonely steeple, majestically silhouetted against the angry sky. At that moment, as has occurred many times in the church's history, a bolt lit the air and thunder boomed, connecting a jagged white line from the clouds to the cross. Nettie jumped back and screamed.

That night Nettie dreamed unsettling visions. They woke her to chills and cold sweat. In one dream, she lived in a glass jar until her life ended. For thirty years, through that transparent prison, she closely observed, but never tasted the fun as rich Charleston life paraded in front of her day after day. In other dreams, she wore stylish fine clothes, bought whatever she wanted, and had gallant lovers visit her from up and down the Eastern seaboard.

All these dreams closed with a frightening vision from the afterlight of the steeple bolt. In the dreams, the struck cross glowed with circulating hot colors. This image coursed with intense physical sensation throughout her mind and body. She woke exhausted and wet, but very much alive.

The next morning Nettie rose early from her bed. She washed, then quietly reflected on her life for a long time before leaving for work. A dove landed on her windowsill. She jumped from her chair and announced to the empty room *"I want more."* She walked straight to her favorite minister's office and resigned her job with the church. The priest eyed her closely. Convinced of her resolution, he asked no questions. "Good luck, Nettie, and God bless you. You are always welcome here."

Only a few days later, in the fall of 1839, Nettie walked inside the Planters Hotel. Countless hungry eyes took in her every aspect: pretty eyes, dark red dress, striking figure, and exquisitely arranged brown hair. She held perfectly still, holding her head high — more out of fright than dignity. She stood there for what seemed like an eternity, but in reality was only a few minutes. A strong man in his early thirties, cradling a glass of whiskey in his big hand, approached her.

"Ma'am, may I help you find someone?"

"No," Nettie replied, "I came here alone."

The man, visiting Charleston from Baltimore, placed his arm in hers and led her to his table.

All around the table were elegant rich men who laughed and told wild tales. In that one night she learned more about business, politics, and the way people lived in other parts of the country than she had in her whole life. She also heard exotic stories about paradise islands in the Caribbean, money and commerce in New York, and the extravagant lives of monarchs in Europe.

Later that night the young man from Baltimore led a wide-eyed Nettie upstairs to his room. She knew what she was there for. The preceding hours had been enthralling, life-giving. These welcome sensations overshadowed whatever awkwardness or shame she felt during the first acts of her new profession.

The Planters Hotel was no common brothel. The women who catered to the rich locals and visiting merchants were the souls of discretion. The hotel functioned from 1809 until the middle of the Civil War as a gentleman's saloon and a fine hotel.

Some men's conduct was less mannerly than others, but on the whole, the high prices charged by the women working the Planters sheltered them from many of the degradations suffered by other Charleston prostitutes, such as those who worked the notorious French Alley brothels that ran between Meeting and Anson Streets.

Within only a few years, Nettie became a wealthy woman. The Planters Hotel flourished. Flush with capital and a growing business, the owners of the hotel had refurbished the entire place in 1835, enabling Nettie's business to ride its wave of ongoing success.

Nettie relished her new financial freedom. Her dreams of exciting lovers, fine clothes, and extravagant living had come true. But over the years, high living and the unorthodox profession she practiced seemed to erode the common sense she once had.

She still attended church every Sunday. Dressed conservatively, she sat quietly in the back and consistently gave a percentage of her earnings to the church. Although the priests had no problem with this, many parishioners did. Charleston's high society women eventually figured out who and what she was. At every opportunity, they snubbed her with disapproving snarls. At first Nettie accepted these rebukes as part of the price she had to pay for what society considered an unacceptable way of life. But over time, the slights made her temper boil. She retaliated in ways that threw the entire parish into social convulsion. Instead of reacting to scornful looks by lowering her head and quickly scurrying out at the end of the service, Nettie began to rush up to her adversaries with open arms, addressing them by name. "Well, hello Mrs. Smith!" she would say. *"You have the most wonderful husband!"*

It did not take long for the people of St. Philip's to realize they had an unusual and dangerous problem on their hands. Instead of actively snubbing her, people took the safer route of avoiding her altogether.

Nettie got angrier. Her antics became more outrageous. She began showing up with out of town clients . . . sometimes two at a time, addressing elite Charlestonians as if they were longtime friends, and wearing inappropriately colorful dresses. Not even the priests wanted to take the chance of upsetting her for fear that she would behave even more outrageously. Nettie soon realized she possessed an odd form of power and it went to her head.

She decided she wanted to put the church itself to the test. To raise money, churches in Charleston at the time allowed prominent parishioners to "buy" specific pews for their families where they would sit every Sunday. Nettie wanted to buy a pew as a physical symbol to publicly elevate her social status.

"You said I would always be welcome," she said one day in the office of the minister she once worked for. "I do not always feel that from people here, but just the same, I give a lot of money to the church."

"That is appreciated Nettie. And despite how some may treat you, I am glad you come."

"You don't really mean that."

"I do, Nettie."

"I am a troublemaker and a lowlife to many."

"You are an equal in the eyes of the Lord."

"All right then," Nettie declared, "prove it."

She outlined her plan to purchase a pew, to have her name on it. She offered a large amount of money, and the priest confirmed it was more than enough.

After looking down at his desk for a long time, rubbing his left earlobe between his thumb and forefinger, the wily priest stood up. "I think we can figure out a way to do this."

Calling on the wisdom earned through years of ministering experience, he held his hand in the air and continued to address Nettie. "You are a clever woman. You know very well that your request puts me in a bad position. But I will make you a bargain and a solemn promise: stop the whoring and you can buy a pew." For weeks afterward, Nettie stood outside before work in the early evening sunlight on the second floor balcony of The Planters Hotel. People coming and going began to take notice of her. She held there, very still, obviously caught in deep thought, staring at the steeple.

An anxious sadness developed in the pit of her stomach. Occasionally she attended church, but more and more frequently, she left feeling tension and resentment. When she happened upon the priest along Church

Street, they nodded cordially to each other; eyes locked in a silent struggle they both knew Nettie was losing.

One day she prayed alone in the expansive nave of the great church. On her way out, she encountered several of the less tolerant parishioners entering the church with the priest. One of the younger and more elegant of the group passed close by her. In a low but steady voice the woman said to Nettie, "This is no place for a whore."

Nettie winced and sought the protection of her priest. When their eyes met, he shut his for a few seconds and took a deep breath. He gazed up at the stained glass windows, then turned and led the group away.

How closely related is the loss of faith in God to the loss of faith in society? The painful immediacy of Nettie's life now rendered such a question useless.

In the weeks following the incident at the church, Nettie's mind spun evermore rapidly within a constricting jar of anger. She worked with great ruthlessness, pushing herself hard to take in greater amounts of money. She never passed at the chance to acknowledge prominent men in front of their wives, whether they were clients of the women who worked the Planters or not. She never again attended church; if she saw the priest walking Church Street, she turned her head.

Although she remained popular with out of town clients, men from Charleston stopped calling on her. Her business suffered because of it, which made her drive to make money strain toward desperation.

People still observed Nettie looking toward the church from the balcony as the sunlight faded away. One evening the priest approached on the sidewalk below her.

"You are no minister," she called down to him.

The priest looked up with an obviously pained expression. He thought for a while. "Nettie, why don't you come see me sometime?"

This time Nettie turned away, shook her head and walked back into the hotel.

The priest did not come see her and Nettie did not visit the priest. Her desperate downward spiral intensified. The charm that once attracted clients to her disappeared into an abyss of anger and volatility. At times, she lashed out at her customers for no apparent reason. When one day, alone on the balcony during a fierce evening thunderstorm, she began ranting wildly, as if enraged at the wind itself, people began to fear her.

From then on, she appeared on the balcony for every evening storm. She held tightly onto the iron railing while the wind whipped at her dress and frayed her long hair backward into an undulating mess. Loud thunder intermittently drowned the sound of her ranting. Sometimes her raving became so disturbing that men in the parlor grabbed her from the balcony. They dried her and placed her into bed while a doctor administered sedatives.

Then, one night in October 1843, storm clouds advanced across the harbor and circled over the peninsula. The wind blew in hard gusts. Nettie made her way onto the balcony and clasped her delicate hands onto the iron railing. Thunder boomed in the distance, and nearby, her old priest made his way down the sidewalk toward her.

As her incoherent wailing became louder, the priest called out to her. She turned to him and denounced him as being more from the devil than from good. Although he genuinely felt for Nettie's plight, he spoke to her in a practiced, perfunctory minister's voice. "Nettie, I want to help you."

When she heard this, she sobbed for several minutes before she looked directly at him, her eyes vacant and cold. "You can't help me," she said in a voice that resonated with overwhelming sorrow. Slowly the fire came back into her eyes. Peering down at him, she shook her head with disgust. "You couldn't anyway."

What the priest saw next emblazoned itself onto his brain for the rest of his life. Nettie stood with her hands clasped at the iron railing, dress blown against her body and whipping behind her. The rain pelted her face. Her matted dark hair twisted wildly in the wind.

Out of a low-lying black cloud, a jagged bolt flashed. The priest instinctively covered his eyes. Just before he did, he witnessed a terrible sight. The lightening touched down onto the hotel's iron railing. The electricity locked Nettie's grip and buckled her knees. Her head thrashed with unnatural force.

The Planters Hotel passed out of existence before the end of the Civil War. The building served in several capacities — as a low rent inn, a grocery store, and a second-hand retail shop — until in 1936 the federal government awarded the City of Charleston a $300,000 Works

Progress Administration grant to restore the building as the Dock Street Theatre. The theater once existed at that location and in nearby spots as early as 1735, well before the Planters came into existence in 1809.

The Dock Street Theatre opened again to great fanfare in 1937 with the same performance that opened it in 1736, "The Recruiting Officer." Later in 1937, and consistently thereafter, theater management as well as guests often witnessed a beautiful but frightening apparition.

A woman in a dark red dress slowly floats through the halls and along the outside balcony of the building's second floor. Her appearance is especially disturbing. She glides down halls and stairways with a zombie-like lack of consciousness. She emerges from walls whole, but transparent and shifting like a continuously fed image from a movie projector. Her eyes are wild and strained open. But the most startling thing about her appearances is that she walks along as if cut off at the knees. Nothing about Nettie Dickerson's life or death could explain this unsettling vision. For years, this aspect of her haunting remained a mystery.

What accounts for it is the fact that during the 1936 renovations, the floorboards of the second floor were raised over twelve inches. Nettie apparently has no consciousness of these changes; she walks the floors of the hotel as they were when she was alive.

In all societies and from the earliest times men have feared the return of the dead. The periodic return of the Dock Street Theatre Haunt strikes fear into those who see her.

Yet, it is the mystery behind the events of her life and death, and how they relate to why she is still condemned to haunt that engenders such a great sense of foreboding. People naturally have a need for clear answers. In this story, there are none. Sometimes the best we can do is to appreciate our blessings, and not be quick to judge other persons. For any one of us, the old saying may prove to have truth to it: "There but for the Grace of God go I."

SUE HOWARD

daughter of the late

R.T. & S.S. WALKER,

wife of

GASTON HARDY,

BORN

Dec. 11, 1856.

DIED

June 16, 1888.

The Spectral Photograph

On the steamy night of June 10, 1987, Charlestonian Harry Reynolds had taken pictures all over the city, capturing a myriad of photographic gems that exist in Charleston after dark. Earlier in the evening he had exhausted the architectural studies that abound in the French Quarter and elsewhere. Now he wanted something more visceral and he thought the graveyard of St. Philip's Church might provide a good opportunity.

The front gates to the graveyard were locked to discourage vagrancy and vandalism. But Reynolds knew how to get closer — he had grown up only a block away on State Street. On that Wednesday night at eleven P.M., Harry crept into the sandy playground that abutted the graveyard. The playground was as empty and quiet as the graveyard. He walked beside the brick wall that divided the two pieces of property, making his way to a beautiful wrought iron gate that allowed passage into the north side of the graveyard. He knew that this gate too would be locked, but it would at least allow his camera lens a closer shot of the slumbering souls in the yard.

Reynolds took a photograph through the ironwork of the gate. He used Kodak ASA-200 film, and although it was new, his camera was not a particularly fancy model.

He aimed it at a row of graves just inside of the gate, focused as well as the limited light would allow on the rounded shapes, and fired. The flash lit the entire grave-yard for one brilliant microsecond.

A few days later Harry eagerly picked up his film. The photos pleased him even though the lack of available light at eleven P.M. made some of the images dark. When he turned to the last picture he had taken that day — the one of the graveyard — he froze. The picture clearly showed the kneeling figure of a translucent woman, garbed in a flowing cloak, in front of one of the head-stones.

Reynolds questioned the photo lab thinking there was a double exposure. He then sent the photograph to Kodak where their scientists verified the authenticity of the picture. They determined it had not been tampered with, and that it was not a double exposure. Reynolds then turned to the task of discovering who it was that knelt in front of that stone monument of his soon to be famous picture.

Aided by his wife and a friend with experience in genealogy, Harry slowly began to research the story of the people whose names and dates were connected to the stone marker in St. Philip's Yard. In time he discovered the gravestone to be that of a woman named Susan Howard Hardy. She had been the young and beautiful wife of Gaston Hardy, the Secretary of the Treasury for the South Carolina Railroad. The prominent couple owned a handsome home at 27 Gadsden Street.

Yet, it was the dates on the monument that Harry

found most startling. Susan Hardy was born on December 11, 1858, and she died on June 16, 1888, at only 29 years old. She died of peritonitis, an infection of the blood caused by complications while she was in labor. Six days before she died, on June 10, 1888, Susan had given birth to a stillborn child.

A chill ran down his spine as Harry Reynolds realized that he had snapped the photograph of Susan Hardy's ghost exactly ninety-nine years to the day of her baby's death.

Mr. Reynolds had captured an image that had burned itself onto the graveyard landscape; the result of a tremendous outpouring of emotion. The loss of a child is perhaps the greatest tragedy in the human experience. Ninety-nine summers before he took the picture, St. Philip's clergy buried a nameless, lifeless infant that should have been Susan Hardy's child. Six days later she joined her baby.

Reynolds captured the spirit of a woman unable to recover from the magnitude of the loss of her child. Like the erosion that carves out canyons over millions of years, an avalanche of sorrow and disappointment has emblazoned her image on that spot.

Echoes of Lament

Farm work outside Newport, Rhode Island planted character and discipline into Joseph Brown Ladd. Meager family finances forced his father to push the boy hard. Early on, Joseph knew there was no hope of happiness to be found there for him, neither in the present with his family nor in a future farming career. So he created his own hope. While working the fields and tending farm animals with a body made solid from physical labor, he developed his mind with imaginative thought. When his father caught him daydreaming, he punished him ruthlessly for it.

Although Joseph continued to work hard for his family, he kept his mouth and mind sealed — his inner self remained a protected sanctuary. As he grew into his teen years, he undertook an extensive course of self-education in a secret place on the far edge of the farm. There, unaware to any other living soul, he designed and built a small shelter in a grove of alder bushes — a study, one that became dense with books on science and literature, and manuscripts of his own poetry. Many blissful hours he spent alone there with his art and books, body idle, and mind enthralled with explorations of fantastical worlds.

One day his father walked to the far edges of the farm to check the terrain for future plowing. While standing in the middle of nowhere, without a soul in sight, he heard whistling. First fear, then amazement, took possession of the farmer. He had always thought the woods in these parts were enchanted and now he had proof: a sprite or elfin being of some kind was in his very midst, filling the forest with a haunting, plaintive music flowing with the zephyr running across tops of trees. Then abruptly, the sprite changed its tune, sounding off with great drama and magic, opening the full resonance of the woods as birds and all manner of forest creatures joined the happy music.

The farmer ran back to tell his wife. He ran into the kitchen wild-eyed and out of breath, but the more he told her about his experience, the more foolish he felt. He stopped describing his charmed experience, and marched back to the remote edges of his land.

His father discovered the sanctuary as he was surveying the land for future planting. He took it as a betrayal and in his initial blind rage, destroyed it with axe and fire. As time went on, the father saw that the effect on the boy was to create an even greater self-containment, a deeper resolve and stilling of the spirit. His father realized he had lost him. So, the destruction of the study proved to separate Joseph even farther in spirit from the farm — the opposite of his father's intention — and resulted in an even earlier physical departure. The study by this time was no longer needed. A much stronger sanctuary now existed in the boy's soul.

Weeks passed. The father watched the boy work the fields, tend to the animals. Rarely was more than a word or two spoken at a time. Finally the father could take the tense silence no more. He approached Joseph.

"What is it Joseph? What is wrong with you? What do you want?"

"Not this."

"Then what? A man must work. Without it, character dissolves. Not to speak of his family going hungry . . ."

"I work," Joseph interrupted, "and I will work. But my future is not in working with my hands. Work that involves my mind is what I want."

As hard as he tried, the father could not suppress a snarl from growing up his lip as he uttered these words: "What do you have in mind, son? Literature? Poetry?"

Joseph stared at him, closely weighing the relationship between him and his father, and realized that absolutely nothing hung in the balance. The interchange ended. The container resealed.

For the son, there was nothing to lose. His father, concerned that he might leave, consented to allowing Joseph to spend two afternoons a week at the Redwood Library in nearby Newport. There, in the library, something happened. A fateful meeting occurred — not his last by any means — that forever changed his life.

As Joseph ambled through the library stacks, memories of his old study in the alder bushes and the idle hours of creative fascination flowed in and through him. They caused him to sigh and stretch with a big smile. Then something off to the left caught his eye. He looked. It was gone. He hurried to the next aisle . . . nothing. But two aisles down, a vision, or so he thought at the time, captured him from the inside out. Its long blonde hair enveloped books that it touched and when it slowly turned its delicate face up to look at him, its sweet blue eyes struck him with strange powers.

Joseph could not remember what happened on that first encounter. He must have turned away or fallen back. When he looked up again, the vision had disappeared and was nowhere in the building.

The experience with the vision endowed his poetry with depth and mystery. Joseph's poetry changed markedly in the week he had to wait for his next visit to the library. No longer did he write the poetry of a trapped adolescent.

Back in the library, he held still, waiting, watching, eyes shifting in all directions. He heard voices down the aisle where he first saw the vision, and advanced toward them. There she was, soft flowing blonde hair, just a girl, holding a book and asking questions to the librarian. Walking nearer, he heard her ask for Spenser's *Faerie Queen*, and thanked God again for the alder bush study. He quoted:

> *All that in this delightfull Gardin growes,*
> *Should happier be, and have immortal bliss.*

Immediately her face beamed with pleasure. A warm joy enveloped Joseph's entire body. In later meetings, they read favorite poetry to each other, and on occasion,

Joseph read his own. Electricity ran through him, and from then on his ears rang whenever Amanda came near.

Joseph asked his father for more time at the library. His father balked until Joseph told him he had a career plan, one that would require his father's assistance. In the many blissful weeks Joseph spent with Amanda, and on the long walks through town, he realized that this woman he wanted as his wife. She desired that he continue to write poetry, but he knew he had to find a means of support for a family.

He decided he could have the blend of art and science he sought in the field of medicine. Sitting by the fire one snowy New England night, Joseph unveiled his plan to his father. Red coals hissed as his father's heart sank. Any remaining hope of Joseph taking over the family business died right there. But the longer he listened the more he observed a young man fully alive. He witnessed a great fire deep within his son, one that eclipsed the surface flickers reflecting from the log flames into the boy's rich brown eyes.

Something physical unlocked in Mr. Ladd's heart. Out came a flood of memories, dreams, and reflections from his own boyhood. His arms and legs tingled. He looked up to see that his son was pleading for help. Some dead part of him, not fully under his control, came alive and grabbed the boy's shoulder, silencing him. "I will help you. I know what to do."

Neither of them spoke again that night. But the father stayed with the boy, flame shadows dancing wildly along walls and ceilings. The big man, with his rough skin and heavy limbs, took the boy's head to his chest and wrapped him in his arms. In that way, the tired boy slept soundlessly through the night.

For the next four years, Joseph studied with his father's friend, the respected Newport physician Dr. Isaac Senter. He still tended to the farm chores, usually in the early hours before the sun rose. The work with Dr. Senter filled his days, and whenever possible, Amanda filled his nights.

Amanda watched her lover persevere in Dr. Senter's office and in the countless hours pouring through medical literature. One night, placing her soft hand in the palm of his, standing close so that he could feel her heat, she spoke softly into his ear, "Joseph, there is no hurry. I am here for you. I will always be here for you." Her words comforted; her body she offered freely as a deep, hot balm.

It was essential to Joseph to achieve doctor status and to open his own practice before he married so that he could provide for his beloved. To Amanda such thinking was unnecessary. The fact was that Amanda was an orphan of rich parents. Her fortune was vast. A guardian, a friend trusted by her parents, administered the proceeds to the estate until Amanda chose to marry.

Joseph believed there should have been no conflict. Dressed in his finest green cloth coat and white shirt frills, he called on the girl's guardian. The man welcomed Joseph. He walked him to the smoking room of the great house, poured glasses of sherry, and listened intently to

Joseph's marriage proposal, then stunned him to the core by rebuking his offer.

Thinking that the man misunderstood his intentions, he approached him again the next morning. The response remained the same. Only this time, the man was unpredictable and rude. The last words echoed inside his head for days. "See Amanda no more."

That evening Amanda came to him, pretty eyes smeared, wet and red. She cried so hard that she could not get words to come out. So Joseph began, "What is wrong with that man? Or what does he find wrong with me?"

"Nothing. That's the danger."

"What do you mean?"

"He's keeping the money, Joseph. He gets to use a certain portion of it each year for himself and his family. That right leaves him when I marry."

"Then it is just a waiting game. And we can talk to lawyers . . ."

"The man is a lawyer, darling. You can bet he has all his dirty bases covered. That is not what concerns me." She paused. "What concerns me is what he will do to paint you to look unsuitable."

The unscrupulous attorney's dark wheels spun evil webs even as the couple spoke. A few days later Joseph encountered strange behavior from patients visiting Dr. Senter's office — they avoided eye contact with him. These encounters multiplied daily.

When it began happening in town shops too, the young man experienced paranoia for the first time in his life. One day, after Dr. Senter and his apprentice applied bandages to seventeen patients and gave herbal medicines to at least seventeen more, the good doctor closed the office door and locked it.

"Joseph, please follow me."

Behind his great oak desk, Dr. Senter explained the situation. It took days for Joseph to completely comprehend what took the doctor only twenty minutes to tell. The gist of it was this: the unscrupulous attorney wielded great power in Newport. And because of the money, he wanted Amanda unmarried for as long as possible. The man would continue to tarnish Joseph's reputation, incrementally stepping up the degrees of slander unless Joseph left town. Joseph's reputation, of course, effected Dr. Senter and his medical practice. The doctor told him that he believed Joseph's aims were pure. Yet, the word around town was that he had taken advantage of young Amanda. He had tricked the innocent girl into loving him, and sought marriage for money.

"You believe this?" Joseph asked the doctor.

The doctor looked away. "No, but Joseph, why didn't you wait until you had your own practice before proposing? Then you would have had a leg to stand on."

Dr. Joseph Brown Ladd first set foot in Charleston under a huge, blue sky on a crisp, clear October day in 1783. Dust-laden, journey worn, with a heart full of love for Amanda in distant Newport, this man brought what the city of Charleston needed — a young doctor willing to work hard. South Carolina did not yet have its own medical college, and the Revolutionary War had taken its toll on the city's supply of medical professionals. At the same time, Charleston prospered. Huge fortunes were being made, the greatest in planting and merchant shipping. Ladd came to the right place to start his new life, free and unencumbered, in a land of riches and wonder. All was new; danger, excitement, and possibility danced together and crackled in the charged October cool.

Joseph's motivation outpaced that of other men in Charleston at that time. His ambition was solely directed. Good-natured and friendly as he was, his mind burned. His heart hurt. Memories of the trickster attorney that guarded Amanda from him and unjustly maligned his character, forcing him to leave Newport, churned not far below the doctor's affable exterior. Some evenings he cried his heart out in tears and in letters written to his love in Newport. Many nights he fell asleep, cheek pressed against the fresh ink of a poem or letter intended for Amanda. In dreams, Joseph saw his golden beloved, reaching for him across water. He ached to feel her heat, to bring her body close to press against his chest. Always he awoke from these dreams feeling sad, warm, and strangely inspired.

During the waking hours, young Dr. Ladd would build the bridge that would bring her to him.

It was on his first day in Charleston that a second chance meeting occurred — one that forever altered the course of his life.

The stagecoach had arrived in the middle of the day at the depot just north of town. Joseph needed a night to rest and clean up before he introduced himself to his only contacts in town — Misses Fannie and Dellie Rose, friends of General Nathaniel Greene, an acquaintance of his father and Dr. Senter. General Greene spent much of the Revolutionary War leading troops in South Carolina. He held the letter of introduction from the General to the Rose sisters tightly as he asked around the depot for directions to a decent inn.

This was the South, a place very different from Newport, and Joseph at first did not know the difference between a man and a fool. Some buffoon masquerading as a man directed him to take a coach over to the Inn at Jones Tavern on Meeting Street. Jones Tavern was a seedy and unsafe place. The fool no doubt had in his head the idea of robbing this finely-dressed and obviously educated young man. But another man, observing from a few yards away, stepped in and took charge of the developing situation. He was tall and cold looking, but his deed was a good one.

"Ralph Isaacs is my name," said the dark-haired stranger, offering a hand to shake. "Clearly you are new here, young man, because this scoundrel has just directed you to a place where you will no doubt be robbed, if not killed."

He stretched out his arm and pointed a long finger at the fool. His voice boomed. "Loose the authorities on this man!" And then, turning his head with confidence toward police that were only in his head, he shouted, "Officer! Officer!"

The thief, under the pressure of Isaac's considerable

personal power, dropped against the wall, panicked, then bolted across the dirt street, tripping over his own ankles and falling flat before disappearing behind a set of horse stables.

Isaacs and the young doctor turned from the pathetic scene and looked at each other. Joseph was the first to crack. Laughing hard, he shook Isaacs's hand again. "I see I owe you a debt, good man. My name is Joseph Brown Ladd, I'm a doctor from Newport, Rhode Island. Tomorrow I call on the Rose sisters at 59 Church Street, but tonight I need a place to sleep and wash-up."

For the rest of that afternoon, Joseph rode with his new friend all over town. Isaacs turned out to be a pushy and insistent man. Despite this, and although all the newcomer really wanted was to get to an Inn and rest, he enjoyed Isaacs, his dry wit, and his presentation of the Holy City. Later, Isaacs brought him to the fine Old Corner Tavern and Inn at Church and Broad Streets, in easy walking distance to 59 Church Street, the Thomas Rose House.

Joseph slept soundly that night. He had no dreams. In the morning, he washed, then put on his best clothes and walked south on Church Street to the Thomas Rose House. He established an immediate connection with the charming Rose sisters. From the start, he ushered life into the house of the bored old ladies. More than that he brought them money by way of rent. But to Joseph, the benefits of the relationship were all his. He got to live in a gorgeous, centrally located Charleston house with two ladies more than willing to mother and nourish him.

They provided meals for him. They were there for him to talk to. He sensed deep levels of trust with them and confided, to them only, the details of the painful story of his love and trials back in Newport. But more than all this, with the help of the Rose sisters Joseph established him-

self far more quickly than was possible for most young men new into town. Social and professional doors flew open. The letter of endorsement from General Nathaniel Greene further secured credibility.

Joseph's connections multiplied. He worked hard and had fun. He and Ralph Isaacs spent a great deal of time together that first year. But as the doctor's practice grew, and his social engagements flourished, the time with Isaacs diminished. In no way did this lessen his regard for the friendship, or for Isaacs the man. Yet, Isaacs at times dropped sarcastic remarks about Joseph being "too important now" to be seen with him. Joseph laughed it off but the comments made him feel bad. If he directed any serious attempts to address the issue, Isaacs just chuckled, slapped his shoulder, and changed the subject.

Demands on Dr. Ladd never deterred him from reserving late evenings for himself. Long solitary walks along the water's edge, moon hung up high over tall mast ships gliding silently out into the Atlantic, some leaving for Northern ports, washed the workday from his mind. All that remained then was a void filled with absolute longing for Amanda. He wanted more than anything to go tearing through the wharves, searching for a ship leaving for the New England coast that would take him to her. Still, the bridge must be built.

Late at night in his room at 59 Church, his mind wandered back through the streets of Charleston in descriptive letters written to Amanda: the yellow glow of ship lights, gas-lit street lanterns reflecting in harbor water, and the cocoon of white, yellow, and pink crepe myrtle tree blossoms that created a flower-cloud heaven over the few blocks surrounding his home.

In poetry, his soul called to her:

> *Ah, think not absence can afford a cure*
> *To the sharp woes-the sorrows I endure.*
> *Amanda, No;'Twill but augment distress*
> *To such a height, no mortal can express.*
> *My soul, distracted, still is fixed on you,*
> *Was ever heart so wretched and so true?*
> From "Arouet to Amanda,"
> *The Literary Remains of Joseph*
> *Brown Ladd, M.D.*

Oftentimes he fell asleep on his writing desk at the

Rose House, exhausted by the tension between the push of professional life and the constant pull of his heart. After the sharply stressful first year of building his medical practice, Amanda again appeared in his dreams. A strong breeze lifted her safely across water to lie close to him. The wind rippled her dress and washed her long golden hair on the sides of his face. This dream filled his whole body with bliss. In it, he held her close against him. She brushed her lips across his, then pressed her soft hands on his cheeks. Drawing closer, she spoke into his ear, "My love, there is time. I am here. I will always be here." Her words comforted. Her body she offered freely as a deep, hot balm.

Joseph woke from these dreams feeling that he inhabited a New World: open, fresh, and clean. The tender words only drove him to work harder, to hasten the day when he could have his love physically with him. Toward the end of his second year in the city, he wrote her guardian, but received no reply.

Evil follows some good men. Evil knows them to be the light bearers that they are, and works to snuff them out. Joseph Brown Ladd was a good man. By this point in his life, the doctor was not naïve to the workings of the dark powers. Events in Newport provided ample reasons for this awakening. He knew Charleston had its darkness too and daily sought to stay aware of it.

As time passed Ralph Isaacs became embittered and insanely jealous of the doctor's success. The first symptom of his insanity had shown itself in guilt-provoking comments couched in smiles and friendly chuckles. Joseph knew in his gut that something was up with the man, but the elusive smiling face cloaked any direct understanding of the developing situation. If he thought about it too much, he felt crazy himself. Trying to understand madness is madness.

Joseph still spent time with his friend. He invited him more and more frequently to social gatherings with elite Charlestonians. Ladd thought that this would resolve the growing tension brewing between them. It only made things worse. Ralph wanted badly to be part of Ladd's social crowd but felt ill at ease once there. The fact is that once Dr. Ladd introduced him around, people accepted Isaacs and invited him to future festivities. The problem was within Ralph Isaacs. Instead of seeing the opportunity life presented him, he resented his friend's social prowess. Resentment gradually turned into stupid, blind anger. That anger warped his mind.

The drama that unfolded in July 1786 between Isaacs and Ladd should never have happened. On July 11, 1786, both men attended a Shakespearean play put on by an accomplished local acting company. The play was Richard III. An amateur actress named Miss Robinson took the role of Queen Anne. The play came off well, but Miss Robinson's inexperience was painfully obvious to the audience.

At intermission, Isaacs met Ladd in the lobby for a drink. His pupils shifted in all directions; never did he look Ladd in the eyes. Biting social remarks flew out of his mouth; nothing Ladd said could calm his rancor. What sent Isaacs over the edge was that in this crowded theater, Ladd sat with his society friends in luxurious box seats, while Isaacs occupied a chair in the hot and stuffy commoner's seating below.

After the play, Ladd walked Isaacs home. Isaacs remained silent. Occasionally he spewed out mean sounding gibberish. Only when Ladd said he enjoyed the performance did Isaacs focus and bite. "How could you say that? The place was hotter than hell! Oh, excuse me. You sat next to the ladies with fans!"

"But Ralph, the performance. Wasn't it fun seeing Shakespeare in Charleston?"

"The acting was awful. And that pathetic woman Robinson. What a sorry excuse for an actress! She ruined the play."

"Come on, Ralph. She's inexperienced. But she's got potential, and she sure is nice to look at."

Ralph stopped, then turned on him. "So that's it! You have interest in her. Your fine South of Broad friends are now introducing you to pretty actresses. I see now. I think I'll write your Amanda about this myself — let her know what you are really about. Ah, but who cares, she's probably off sleeping with some actor in Newport anyway!"

Isaacs snarled, ready to brawl. Ladd took a deep breath, fighting back a surge of rage. Until that moment, he was unaware of how much tension festered within him from the past months of dealing with Isaac's growing derangement. He stuck out his hand. "Good night Ralph."

Isaacs glared at the hand as if it were a clump of horse feces. He spat, turned, and marched into darkness.

Somewhere in the course of that night Ralph Isaacs crossed the border of sanity and did not come back. In the weeks that followed, any attempts by Ladd to contact him were rebuked. Worse yet, Isaacs began an open slander campaign against Ladd that intensified daily. The doctor knew of it, but only after enormous pressure from friends did he act against it. In a letter printed in a column of the October 12, 1786 *Charleston Morning Post and Daily Advertiser,* he stated, "I account it one of the misfortunes of my life that I ever became friends with such a man."

Not surprisingly, given his state of mind, Isaacs published a reply on October 16: "I dare affirm that the event of a little time will convince the world that the self-created doctor is as blasted a scoundrel as ever disgraced humanity."

Today Dr. Ladd might have found the strength to cast aside such personal defamation as the ravings of a madman. But those were the days of Chivalry, the Code of Honor, that invisible chain binding all who cared to matter in society. In those times, men settled matters of honor in duels.

Again, Joseph Brown Ladd found himself locked into the tense battle between society's vulgar manipulations and the call of his heart. This time, the complexity of the matter deepened. A duel translated into possible death, meaning no union with Amanda in this lifetime. And yet, no duel meant a blatant lack of defense of his character, honor, and integrity. Back in Newport, he had been a child with no real weapon or choice against the blind ruthless power of an attorney who sought to ruin him to benefit from Amanda's money. In Charleston, he was an adult with choices. And the choice must be to keep his life in Charleston clean and unspoiled for the coming of his beloved.

He challenged Isaacs to a duel.

The entire night before the dreaded dawn duel hour he wrote to Amanda. The poems of that night speak loudly for what the man was going through:

> *Death, friendly death may soon relieve my pain.*
> *Long, sure, he cannot be implored in vain.*
> *Soon, the grim angel will restore my peace,*
> *Soothe my hard fate, and bid my sorrows cease*
> *And tear Amanda's image from my breast.*
>
> *When deep oblivion wraps my mind in night,*
> *When death's dark shadows swim before my sight,*
> *Will, then, Amanda? Ah, she will I trust,*
> *Pay the last tribute to my clay-cold dust.*
> *Will, sighing, say, there his last scene is o'er.*
> *Who loved as mortal never loved before.*
>
> *O'er my lone tomb oh, yield that sad relief,*
> *Breathe that soft sigh and pour out all your grief,*
> *Or, shed one tear in pity as you pass,*
> *And just remember that your Arouet was.*
> From *The Literary Remains of*
> *Joseph Brown Ladd, M.D.*

The knock at the door came shortly before dawn. The Rose sisters escorted Joseph onto Church Street, friends led him the rest of the way to open fields near what is Line Street today. Isaacs already stood in position, the tail of his long black jacket flipping up behind him in the breeze. Joseph wanted to cry out to Ralph, to appeal to the part of this person who first befriended him, and to the memory of cherished times together. But when he looked up to speak to the man, he saw eyes that were vacant.

The seconds checked the pistols, turned the men back to back, and placed the guns into the palm of each right hand. The twenty-one step march began. Between steps ten and twenty, the urge to kill Isaacs rose and flashed into far corners of his brain. Then appeared soft Amanda, radiant against the dawn sky, opening her arms for him. Eyes smeared, wet and red, she called out, "Joseph, I am here." At step twenty-one he turned, and discharged his pistol into the sky.

Isaacs held his gun steady, took his time. He aimed first at the head, then stopped at the heart. At the last second he lowered the gun and blasted at the knees.

On that fateful day, Ralph Isaacs, at the last minute, acted not to kill Ladd but to cripple him for life.

That is not how it turned out. Joseph spent his last days in the second floor room at the top of the stairs at 59 Church Street. No doctor could save him. The wounds were too severe. Charleston medical professionals and the Rose sisters gave him their best care. Yet, it was not their comfort he sought. When conscious, he pleaded to every-one entering that room to bring him Amanda. And in delirium caused by fever and gangrene, his howl for her echoed into homes throughout the neighborhood.

The Rose sisters dispatched letters to Amanda to come quickly. They were to no avail. Her guardian kept her locked away, barring her from joining Joseph in his final days.

Dr. Joseph Brown Ladd died in that room without his beloved Amanda. As all bodies eventually do, his failed and was buried. The good doctor's soul left for heavens beyond the flower-clouds South of Broad Street. But some aspect of his gentle spirit stays in Charleston. It inhabits the house and grounds of 59 Church Street, often appearing during times of confusion, sickness, or emotional trial. By all accounts he is tall with brown hair, good-looking, and dressed in fine late eighteenth-century clothes. This ghost is slow to action. His eyes search, his facial expression caught in deep thought. He observes the house while strolling outside through the lush lawn and gardens. Frequently, in either day or night, his footsteps are heard, moving slowly and heavily up and down three flights of stairs.

Sometimes the whistle of a delighted sprite moves through the dark-wooded rooms of the old house, followed by the whimpers of a sad and lonely little boy. And in cracking thunderstorms and at times even during the most gentle of rains, loud echoes of a man pleading for his love to come to him are silenced by a soft feminine hush, "I am here."

Fire Station #8

Great fires blazing through Charleston account for more destruction since 1670 than war, hurricane, or earthquake combined. Until the twentieth century, firefighters lacked the equipment to effectively combat firestorms.

Through the 1700s Charlestonians constructed mostly wood dwellings and commercial buildings. Firefighting citizens formed long water bucket brigades, a valiant but minimally effective weapon against the fast fury of flames devouring dry wood. Occasionally gunpowder proved effective. Sometimes officials detonated entire homes. They blasted gaps between buildings, often successfully stopping the spread of flame.

As early as 1698, a fire destroyed some fifty dwellings. Other early major fires on record include ones in 1699, 1700, and 1731. The most catastrophic blazes were those of 1740, 1838, and 1861.

A section of the 1852 Directory of the City of Charleston titled "Fires in Charleston" begins:

> It is curious and interesting to contemplate the numerous fires which have occurred in the city of Charleston — to mark the destruction of property

— to witness the elasticity of the inhabitants . . . the amount of suffering in time past, from this cause . . . would appall the stoutest heart; and yet the spirit of the citizens has never been subdued or broken down by any of these calamities.

This directory describes in detail fires from the one on January 15, 1778, which destroyed nearly half of Charleston, including the entire Charleston Library and its 6,000 volumes. According to the 1852 Directory, in the 1838 blaze:

> One-third of the city, 145 acres . . . *one thousand one hundred and fifty-eight buildings* (Italics added) were destroyed . . . The City Council very promptly and wisely enacted a law . . . which requires that all buildings . . . shall be constructed of brick or some other incombustible material.

Despite these preventive measures, the worst was yet to come. The Great Fire of 1861's destruction dwarfed all by comparison.

At 8:30 P.M. on December 11, 1861, fire bells rang throughout the city. An ominous red lantern in St. Michael's steeple, hanging on a pole, pointed northeast, toward the fire. Powerful northeasterly winds made it impossible to contain. The December 13, 1861 *Charleston Courier* reported that "Keeping on in a course, the roaring element rushed through [city blocks] almost liked forked lightning."

Two days later the fire hissed out at the west end of Tradd Street after destroying 540 acres of the most densely populated part of the city. The Charleston diarist Emma Holmes witnessed the destruction:

> The scenes all along the streets were indescribably sad. The pavements loaded with furniture, clothing and bedding of refugees who cowered beside them in despair, while others were hurrying with articles for safety . . . When we reached the Battery, the wind was so high we could scarcely breast it. The heavens black as midnight while the waves were white with foam and all illuminated by the intense lurid light.
>
> Throughout that awful night, we watched the weary hours at the windows and still the flames leaped madly on with demonic fury, and now the spire of our beautiful Cathedral is wrapped in flames. There it towered above everything, the grandest sight I've ever beheld; arch after arch fell in, and still the cross glittered and burned high over all. Then the roof caught and we saw that too fall in. *At five the city was wrapped in a living wall of fire from the Cooper to the Ashley without a single gap to break its dread uniformity.* (Italics added) It seemed as if the day would never dawn. Oh, it was the longest, weariest night I ever spent . . .

A month after the fire Emma recorded what it was like to walk through the burnt district by moonlight:

> . . . It seems as if we were carried centuries back and stood among the ruins of some ancient city. How desolate seemed the few solitary houses still standing . . . Nothing but ruins on every side; it is more dreary than living by a cemetery. We walked where once our beloved home stood, and, as we listened to the passing sound of the oarsmen and their

songs and the chimes of old St. Michael's bells, they seemed to ring clearer through the silence which reigned above. The moonlight was brilliant.

Charleston remains vulnerable to fire because of how close the old buildings are to each other. However, soon after the fire of 1861 the city began to implement measures to prevent further catastrophes. In 1877, Charleston installed an advanced system of station circuits and call boxes throughout the city. Fire towers were constructed with huge warning bells. Finally, in January 1882, Charleston created a city department of professional firefighters. Station #8 on Huger Street came into existence in 1910 in an ongoing expansion of the department.

Somewhere in the recesses of Huger Street Firehouse #8 lurks a violent and sinister presence. On the second floor one room stretches the entire length of the building. Firemen on duty sleep there.

Ten iron-framed beds line up in a perfect row through the center of the room; two more at the top front end stick out from the wall at right angles from the others. A long-planked hardwood floor provides the sparse room with a sense of permanence and strength. It shines like the massive red fire engine parked below.

Because the firemen work in shifts, the sleeping quarters always remain dark. During the day, only the thinnest shards of bright light pierce the outer edges of the thick window blinds. At night blackness so thoroughly blankets the room that wide-open eyes jerk in vain for traction in the absolute dark.

Engineer Jack deTournillon worked at Fire Station #8 from April 17, 1989 until he got promoted and moved out July 10, 1992. For three months he worked at the station without incident. Then on July, 17, 1989, a series of bizarre and frightening events transpired that would leave Jack forever changed in his feelings toward the unknown.

At 3 A.M. on that July morning deTournillon woke to the sound of faint voices in the distance. Since he slept near the Huger Street end of the upstairs dormitory, he dismissed the noise as that of people walking past the station. But as the volume increased, he soon realized that he was hearing the sound of deep conspiratorial voices, disembodied chants from men plotting in a strange tongue. Pressure built in the room, making it difficult for him to breathe. A breeze swirled around his head.

He shook his head hard. The breeze stopped and the pressure receded. The voices quieted and the groggy firefighter, breathing easy now, shifted in his bed and drifted back toward slumber.

Moments later the voices came back, chanting with menace and increasing volume. The swirling breeze blew again, this time sweeping from the foot of the small iron bed along the sheets to blow past his head up against the wall.

DeTournillon tried to leap from his bed. At that moment the attack began. A force grabbed him by the waist and roughly drove him toward the floor. He caught himself at the edge of the bed and pushed himself back to the middle. Lying on his back, he peered into the darkness, searching for clues to help him understand what was happening.

Then, an overwhelming force fell upon his body and drove him deep into the bed. He lay there struggling, pinned and helpless, trying in vain to yell out for help. Fellow firefighters lay peacefully asleep only twenty feet away from him, but the unnatural power had rendered him speechless.

The force jolted his head to the left and held it there. All he could see was the next bed, but his entire attention was focused on the void above his body where he knew something horrifying was suspended, invisible, but just inches away from his face.

A painful, heavy weight pressured his chest. His arms flipped up so that his hands, now near his shoulders, locked into a position to press upward. He pushed with all his might — in vain.

He tried again. He pushed for what seemed an eternity, fighting the enormous weight until he slowly began to overpower it. The attacking force released a loud, struggling growl then fell way. For seconds it still hovered over and around Jack's bed. Then it sprang far back, disappearing into the deep recesses of the room.

DeTournillon, now free but dazed and in a cold sweat, listened to the comforting whir of the air conditioning unit. Firemen snored peacefully in beds just a few yards away.

His heart pounded in his chest. A sharp scraping noise cracked through the room. Reality hit him. He leapt out of bed, swearing loudly. He banged his locker door wide open, startling the other men from sleep. He gathered his belongings, marched down the stairs, still cussing and swearing, ready to leave the station.

The other firemen followed him down the stairs to find out what happened. As he told them about the encounter, they gathered at the bottom of the stairway that led to the second floor. They stood, listening to Jack, watching the closed door. The temperature where they stood dropped twenty degrees. They all recognized what the chill meant. The presence was still there.

Days later deTournillon again assumed duty at the station. When night fell, Jack went upstairs, hoping to conquer his fear. But that night he could not sleep. Over the next year and a half, the invisible force would challenge him a dozen more times, each time at exactly 3 A.M.

Jack deTournillon says that none of the subsequent visitations were as violent as the first. Some nights the force hovered over the bed and left as Jack became aware of it. At other times, he heard it walk well past the bed and then back again.

Each visit was memorable, but the last sticks with him the most. The menacing entity used the same deep growling voice of the first encounter. It called his name, "Jack!"

For two years the authors of this book searched in vain for clues as to the source of the haunting in Firehouse #8. First we studied the McCrady plats (Charleston surveyor collections spanning nearly 300 years) speculating that the building might have been built on an old Indian or African-American graveyard. Next we researched fire histories as far back as 1698. The most interesting research material came from the sixteen fire-

men we interviewed. Eight of them had experienced the entity repeatedly.

In one group interview, we stood with the firemen at the base of the stairs, listening to these strong working men of Charleston tell their fantastic stories. They pointed up at the door to the sleeping quarters. Several of them periodically wrung their hands and rubbed the goosebumps on their arms, chilled by the overwhelming weight of supernatural testimony.

As they continued their stories, a cold, physical dread enveloped all of us, permeating the immediate vicinity. We tried to remain professional about it, not wanting to reveal our alarm to the superstitious firemen. Within seconds, the temperature for a full yard out from the first stair dropped more than twenty degrees — a startling occurrence in the middle of a hot Charleston day in August. For us, it verified firsthand one of the many disturbances common to this location.

Still, the source of it all remained a mystery.

We decided to call in a great national resource, who now lives in Charleston. The gifted visionary and psychic consultant Elizabeth Baron has achieved spectacular success in her twenty-one years as a professional medium. We had heard of her accomplishments and national reputation well before beginning to write this book. Yet we remained skeptical. Some of our reservation was a healthy professional detachment, and some of it was flat out avoidance. We pictured her as a flamboyant Hollywood show woman, talented in employing "spiritual" theatrics, but probably lacking authenticity.

To our surprise we found Elizabeth Baron to be a humble woman. She exudes a calm strength. Her demeanor is gentle and her focus seems to be genuinely toward service to others, but there is something elusively disconcerting about her.

What is unsettling is that in her, two wildly disparate but fully developed personality traits seem to co-exist in harmony. She speaks with worldly experience and childlike vulnerability *at the same time*. The effect is arresting. Rather than falling into a dreamy state of relaxed acceptance, we found that listening to her threw us into a heightened, edgy awareness.

Over the years Ms. Baron has successfully assisted dozens of police departments, the Secret Service, the FBI and the military in investigations that would not have had a resolution without her. Her scrapbook is filled with official and unofficial letters of commendation from these sources. She has thousands of clients, including regular working people, international diplomats, medical doctors, and Hollywood movie stars.

She has appeared on national television shows and at one time had her own radio show in Nevada that reached fifteen states, Canada, and Mexico. She is currently working with the producer Tracy Reiner, daughter of Rob Reiner and Penny Marshall, on a movie about her life story called "The Visionary."

On August 28, 1999 we led Elizabeth, two of her men assistants, and Jack deTournillon into the second floor of

Firehouse #8. Elizabeth began the channeling session with a prayer for protection and guidance. She opened her Bible at random to Ezekial and read a passage that was particularly unsettling that day because, as she spoke, powerful Hurricane Dennis churned its way up the Gulfstream toward Charleston.

Ezekial 27, from the *Living Bible* paraphrased by Tyndale:

> But now your statesmen bring your ship of state into a hurricane. Your mighty vessel flounders in the heavy eastern gale and you are wrecked in the heart of the seas. Everything is lost; your riches and wares, your sailors and pilots, your shipwrights and merchants and merchants and soldiers and all the people sink into the sea on the day of your vast run.
>
> All your sailors out at sea come to land and watch upon the mainland shore, weeping bitterly and casting dust upon their heads and wallowing in ashes. They shave their heads in grief and put on sackcloth and weep for you in bitterness of hearts in deep mourning.

She said that the main purpose of her channeling sessions was to bring useful information about life after life to people — those living and those who have passed on but not yet gone into the light. She said she hoped our book might serve some of the same purpose. She asked the Creator of the Universe to use her as an instrument, adding that if indeed there were disturbed spirits present that they be led to the light of God.

She stretched out on one of the twelve unmade steel-frame beds. Her assistants clicked on a video recorder as Elizabeth took in a series of deep inhalations. After several minutes her body stiffened slightly, then relaxed. Soon after her breathing steadied and the atmosphere of the entire room changed. Physically Elizabeth and the room looked the same. But the air felt charged—the hair on our heads rose slightly as if lightening were about to strike.

The next time Elizabeth spoke it was not Elizabeth. The entity speaking through her announced that she was Saint Catherine of Sienna, grateful to be of service. One of the assistants, Jim Smyre, a lanky, studious looking man in his early fifties greeted Saint Catherine in a serious, booming deep voice.

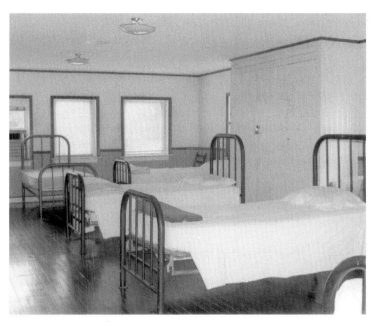

✦

"Good evening Saint Catherine. We are here in Firehouse #8 in Charleston. What has brought us together is some indication of a psychic impression, disturbance or a free-floating entity in this building. What we are here to determine is . . . what is this? What can we do about it? Who can we help cross into the light? We welcome any information you can give us, particularly concerning what we should learn from this and what we might be able to teach others."

Saint Catherine responded immediately.

It is very important for the teachings about ghost phenomenon to be distributed in the world at this time. Many people laugh at or play with this phenomenon in a dangerous way.

There are spirits everywhere. Some are people who have passed into the spirit realm, have gone to the light of God and come back as God-appointed saints and angels to guide and to lead the living.

There are also those who have not gone to the light of God. They do not know they are dead. They are confused and can interfere with the living in negative ways.

Before bringing Elizabeth Baron into the firehouse, we gave her no information about the place other than that we believed it to be haunted. Catherine of Sienna told us that the disturbed spirit in the firehouse was that of an overweight, sixty-eight-year-old fireman who died of emphysema and a bad heart.

The man has not faced the fact that he is dead. He had a miserable home life. His wife complained constantly and nagged him for fifty years. This spirit lives in this building, the only place he found pleasure and happiness in life. He does not mean to be a dark presence. He is at present a lost soul.

He was a big man with curly, salt and pepper colored hair. When not on the second floor, he can be seen continually walking up and down the stairs. He is never at rest.

This man hated to go home. He loved being here with the men. He often spent many hours after a work shift walking the stairs, worrying about what he would have to deal with when he got home. Firehouse #8 was his haven . . . he lived for this place and for the important work he performed for the city.

"Catherine," the serious assistant with the big voice asked, "when the men of this fire station experience this spirit, it can be a terrifying experience. What can they do to prevent this or to protect themselves?"

Yes, this spirit can manifest his fear, confusion, and negativity to living people. Usually it will happen at night when defenses are down. This spirit can transfer his fear and confusion, mentally and physically, to the people working and sleeping here. He will mostly manifest around their face to get their attention.

In such instances it is best to say out loud "I fear no evil, for Thou art with me" then repeat the Lord's Prayer several times. Tell the spirit that the fear and pain are his, not yours. Tell him that he does not need to feel pain anymore. Encourage him to move toward God's light.

Jack deTournillon spoke up and said that twice the hauntings were accompanied by many voices speaking at once.

"That is just the spirit world," Catherine answered him. "These are special men employed here. These are people whose work takes them close to the spirit realm. It is not unusual for them to see destruction and death firsthand. Hearing the voices from the spirit world is not uncommon for people in jobs like this."

We asked, but Catherine did not tell us, the name of the fireman whose spirit now haunts Firehouse #8. We did find pictures of men now deceased who were once employed there that fit the description she gave us. It may be that she did not know his name. Or possibly there was a reason she did not tell us. We concluded that whatever the case, it was best for us to let it rest.

Toward the end of our time with Elizabeth, we all gathered in a circle and prayed that the entity haunting that place would find his way to peace and rest.

We asked Catherine if there was anything more we could do to be of service through writing this book. She left us with the following words:

Bring truth. Teach that ghosts are people and whenever possible, to be compassionate with them. As long as Charleston holds onto its many ghosts and does not encourage them to go to the light, the city is in danger.

The presence of these spirits effects the residents of homes and other buildings. People can take on the ghosts' distorted personalities, all their horrible madness and pain. This agony can even extend to taking on their same death . . .

For instance, there could be a young woman who hanged herself in a building and still existed there, trapped between worlds. Later, if a living woman suffering from depression spent time there, then this person would be highly vulnerable.

The depressed person then not only tunes into the depression in herself, but also to the pain and negativity generated by the disembodied entity. In this way the spirit can influence her toward the same death.

This is what we call possession. Possession is alive and well today, as it has been throughout civilization.

These are things the public needs to know.

The Cooper River Bridge

Late one Sunday afternoon in February 1966, a Charleston family of five advanced over the old Cooper River Bridge toward Charleston, returning from a weekend at their Sullivan's Island family beach house on Marshall Boulevard. They rode in a dark blue 1965 Pontiac station wagon, a very wide car by today's standards, and it seemed especially so on the narrow lanes of what is formally known as the John P. Grace Memorial Bridge.

While the father guided the car higher and higher toward the great bridge's summit, expansive harbor views called to him. He stole glances to the left far out over the water and then ahead to watch the peninsula wonders unfold beneath him the higher he climbed.

The highest point of steel on the bridge is 270 feet over the water. The thinnest points of steel are the guardrails that stand as flimsy reminders that there is little protection from launching, at the least, over 150 feet through the air toward high-speed impact with the Cooper River.

The road ahead of him was clear. Still, strong winds required a steady hand at the wheel and cut short his taking in the stunning views as he turned his attention back to the road after a big gust of wind shook his car.

And then it happened. Not forty yards ahead of him, an old green sedan slammed on its brakes. He immediately crunched down on his own brakes, then shouldered hard into the left lane. As it turned out, he was in no danger. The old car never stopped, it continued rolling along ahead of him. He figured the same gust of wind that made him brace caused the driver ahead to cautiously hit his own brakes.

Upon closer inspection, the family man identified the car ahead of him as a 1940s-era sedan in excellent condition. The same number of people traveled in it as in his own — a family of five. The old sedan rambled along slower than the speed limit. He decided to pass it.

As he passed the dark car, his wife, seated beside him, commented how strangely the people in the old car were dressed and how odd and expressionless they all looked, especially the children. Then the wind rushed hard and the cheeks of the man driving the old sedan blanched white; extreme alarm rushed through his entire countenance, and he swerved toward the Pontiac. The tires of both cars screeched, but only the Pontiac came to a full stop. A foghorn blared. The old sedan lunged forward and after advancing a short distance farther up the bridge, it totally vanished from sight.

A similar experience happened to Harriet Langston of Charlotte, North Carolina, in 1996, soon after she had moved to Charleston. Her new Honda Sport Civic shot up the old Cooper River Bridge like a white bullet. The small lanes never bothered her in this compact car, and her confidence in Japanese engineering allowed her to cruise the narrow bridge at well over 55 miles per hour without even thinking about it. The Civic climbed the bridge's first tower just after dark one windy, cloudy evening. Well ahead of her, she saw several cars rise to the bridge crest under the gigantic silver trestles and then drop out of sight as they started to descend on the other side of the summit. She quickly caught up to the car nearest to her.

At first, she paid little attention to it, preparing to speed past it in the left lane. Yet, the closer she got to it, the more fascinated she became. The car was a green antique Oldsmobile with wide black tires and a rounded back. As she pulled alongside, she slowed to get a closer look at the unusual automobile. What she saw next nearly caused her to flip her own car over the rails.

Five people rode in the car: a whole family, dressed in clothing and hair styles from somewhere in the first half of the twentieth century. Two children sat in the back seat with an elderly lady. A man drove the car, a young woman sat on the passenger side. All stared ahead blankly, devoid of animation, until the head of the driver slowly turned left to look out the window toward her. His face was totally expressionless, colored white with unearthly pallor, eyes sunk so far back into his head that she could not see them. Fright jolted her; she hit the brakes and let the Oldsmobile ride on. For a few seconds more, she watched it climb higher and higher then slowly disappear as if into a fog bank.

◆

What is happening on the aging Grace Memorial Bridge in these and other similar reports is a profound mystery. It is unexplainable in material, causal terms.

Yet the contemporary connection with a green 1940 Oldsmobile sedan and the Cooper River Bridge's most horrifying disaster is unmistakable.

On February 24, 1946, the World War II-era freighter *Nicaragua Victory* moved from its moorings in Charleston Harbor to the Wando River near Hobcaw Point. The engines were shut down and the anchor dropped.

The ship had been anchored in the harbor for two days awaiting repairs from an accident in Saudi Arabia. The captain ordered the ship moved to this new location, about a mile upstream from the Grace Memorial Bridge, to be closer to shipyards and for extra protection from impending bad weather.

Jesse R. Morillo, twenty-three years old at the time, served as an engine room oiler on the Nicaragua Victory. In an interview published in the February 25, 1998 *Post and Courier*, Morillo remembered that:

> the trouble began . . .when the weather turned sour and began buffeting the ship. The ship's night captain ordered the boatswain to drop another anchor. Then, he ordered that some slack be taken up in the anchor chain. Instead, the boatswain accidentally winched both anchors out of the mud. In no time, all 12,000 tons of the *Nicaragua Victory* was floating downstream sideways at 3 to 5 mph. With the engines shut down, there was no steering or stopping it. . . . the ship's bow, which pointed [east, away

sents
n Job

Ira
De

Tehr...
Stand...

CAR TAKEN FROM COOPER — The automobile of the ... as the Salmons company was removing bridge wreckage. A Elmer Lawsons, which went through the broken John P. 240-foot girder span had not been removed from the approach Grace Memorial bridge the afternoon of February 24 when made place where the car was being when a huge grappling the Nicaragua Victory rammed the structure and took out a bracket caught hold of its rear bumper. Divers previously 240-foot section during fresh high winds, is shown [above] had abandoned efforts to locate the car pending removal of as it was recovered yesterday afternoon by the Salmons the wreckage. Bodies of Mr. and Mrs. Lawson, two neighbor Dredging company. Captain Harry V. Salmons, head of the Mrs. Rose Lawson, and the Lawsons two children, Robert S. company, is shown hatless at the left. The car was located and Doris 2, were found in the car. (Photo by Rollin ...)

from Charleston] toward the Mount Pleasant side, became stuck in the mud shortly before the ship arrived at the bridge. The effect was like a slingshot, or a pivot, as the ship's stern picked up speed.

High up over the panic and drama unfolding on the river below, three vehicles climbed the bridge's first tower: two automobiles and an Army mail truck. As the first car made it past the two-thirds mark up the first tower, the stern of the 12,000 ton *Nicaragua Victory* struck one of the bridge's main pillars and tore into the multi-faceted bottom support trestles.

According to Morillo, "The spans did not fall right away" and the bridge remained intact for three minutes after impact. Then all hell began to break loose and Morillo and other crewmembers dove for cover as four-foot bridge rivets ricocheted through the air and hit the deck.

The first car on the bridge sped on toward Charleston. Just as the first of three 100-foot sections dropped out of sight, that first car left the collapsing segments and crossed to safety, never stopping until reaching solid pavement on the peninsula, the driver knew that at any time, more of the bridge might come down.

The Army mail truck, the last of the three vehicles, braked in the middle of the bridge. The driver did not bother reversing the truck but instead, leapt out of it and fled wildly back down the bridge.

Between these two vehicles was a green, 1940 Oldsmobile carrying Elmer R. Lawson, his wife, Evelyn, his mother Mrs. Rose Lawson, his seven-year-old son Robert and his two-year-old daughter Diane.

After the ship's impact, "I saw him stop, then start, then stop and start again," Morillo says, describing how the driver reacted. "If he'd kept on going, he'd have made it across."

As the bridge began to come down, much of the first two sections fell across the deck of the *Nicaragua Victory*. The third and highest section, the one furthest from the stern, crashed fully into the water. The green 1940 Oldsmobile plunged with it, all five of the Lawsons still in it, slamming into the cold February water and plummeting straight to the dark bottom of the Cooper River.

A diving team dispatched to locate the car eventually gave up. The car remained in the Cooper River from February 24, 1946 until March 19, 1946 when the jaws of a huge grappling bucket dredging the river bottom and lifting chunks of bridge span wreckage out of the water, caught hold of the car's rear bumper and lifted it into the air. All five bodies were still in the car.

Another freak accident occurred only days after the Lawson tragedy. Forty-one-year-old Marshall Cleveland, part of the construction crew restoring the bridge after the *Nicaragua Victory* catastrophe, fell headfirst into the fresh concrete being poured to build up a damaged pillar. Cleveland was buried alive by thousands of pounds of wet cement. His body rests quietly, entombed as part of the great structure itself.

The *Nicaragua Victory* accident is one of the saddest stories in modern Charleston history. Despite the tens of thousands of ships that have passed under the bridge since 1946, and under the newer Cooper River Bridge that runs parallel to it (the Silas Pearman, built in 1965), such a catastrophe has fortunately not been repeated. Yet, many people believe that the dilapidated old bridge, still in daily use, is currently an impending disaster, that it is a tragedy in the making even without a 12,000-ton tanker slamming into it. While political posturing continues, the old bridge holds on. But no man-made structure can hold forever.

Sensational disasters such as the 1946 accident with the *Nicaragua Victory* and the Cooper River Bridge become charged pockets of consciousness on the collective psyche of a community. Such charged pockets of psychic energy may account for the sightings of the ghostly 1940 Oldsmobile sedan reported to still travel toward the city on the old bridge.

The experience of the great bridges captivates the imagination and embeds itself deep into the psyche of those whose lives it touches. The Cooper River Bridge appears frequently in the dreams and daydreams of countless Charlestonians, and even among people who have only visited the city. Sometimes these dreams are majestic and soaring and ecstasy filled. From on high the dreamer watches the great timeless drama unfold: the Holy City transforms — all the passion and love, all the creation and destruction of the centuries wheel by, glowing, grinding, and wailing in absolute silence.

At other times the bridge's dark side manifests: the dreamer finds himself stuck at the top, alone on a skybound steel bridge trestle with nothing to grasp but the wind, a slippery silver trestle, and the pull of a terrifying expanse of water far below.

Sometimes in these dreams, the ghosts of the dozens of suicide jumpers, with their sad faces and broken psyches, call out to us, imparting information that in their mortal psychic hell they could not tell us. These suicides are people we know, part of the Charleston community. On the trestle, we find that we are not alone. The spirits of those who have died there, still longing, yet shed of mortal anguish, lead us by the hand to safety, imparting one resolute command: "Live."

Heartfelt appreciation to Sue Flaster.
Without her stalwart presence,
this book would not have been published.

Special thanks to Vance Grady, Susan Hayes, John Ingram,
Leroy Jackson, Bob Moore, Julian T. Buxton, Jr.,
the staff at Tour Charleston LLC
(especially Laurens Smith and Adam Artigliere),
and Jim Buxton.

Our families
Jane Dog
Stanley and Arthur
    (Eddie's Bassets)
Cathy Forrester
Jon and Betsy Anderson
Frank and Cecilia Gruber
Tom, Henry, and Molly Fair
Mary Pope Hutson
Richard Ross
Andrew Nock
Eddie Fava
Reggie Gibson
Ann and Charles Ailstock
Amy McPhail
Donald McPhail
Jane Floyd and the other
    wonderful people who kept
    us fed at the 1837 Bed and
    Breakfast
Sherry Weaver and Rick Duhn
Drayton and Kat Hastie and the
    great staff at the Battery
    Carriage House Inn
Betsy and Buddy Jenrette
Robin and Joyce Hitchcock
Jon Poston

Katherine Saunders
Leigh Handel
Valerie Perry and the staff of the
    Aiken-Rhett House
Grahame Long
Ainsley Fisher
Lee Lewis
Ashley Watson
Molly Maloney
Malcolm Hale
George Geer
Travis Landrith
Ed Pugh
Suzy Uzdavinis
Kristy Genthner
Geordie Buxton
Mel White
Ruth Burts
Nenutzka Villamar
Amy Ballenger
Helen Hill
Charleston Area Convention
    and Visitors Bureau
Charleston Metro Chamber of
    Commerce
Lowcountry Open Land Trust
Wade Kersey

USC Small Business Resource
    Development Center
Historic Charleston Foundation
Charleston Library Society
Charleston County Library,
    especially the staff of the
    South Carolina Room
The Preservation Society
Grace Episcopal Church
The City of Charleston
Charleston Fire Department
Robin McCain
Nancy Smythe
Bobbie Ball and Poogan's Porch
    Restaurant
Charles Ball
Dan Petterson
Frank Palmer
Lynn Barlow
Alice Genthner
Jack deTournillon and all who
    have served at Station #8
Elizabeth Baron
Eric Pedersen
Roger Pinckney
Michael Meads Design
Karen Phillips
Robert Phillips
Anne Buxton
Anne Daniell

James McPherson
Liz Buxton
Kaye Graybeal
Dino Copses
Hap Cooper
Dr. Nan Morrison at the
    College of Charleston
Kay Motley at Old South
    Carriage Company
Jimbo McAlister
The *Post & Courier* Archives
    Department
Mindy Spar
Susan Hill Smith
Mike Macy and Pastime
    Amusement Company
Dr. Norman Olsen
Venable "Starsky" D. Wilson
Archie Willis at McAlister-
    Smith Funeral Home
The Deerys
Bruce Springsteen
Walker Percy
Norman Cousins
James Dickey
Pat Conroy
The many unmentioned people
    who have told us their
    stories.

Selected Bibliography

BOOKS

Andrews, Sidney. *The South Since the War*. New York: Arno Press, 1969.

Burton, E. Milby. *The Siege of Charleston, 1861–1865*. Columbia: University of South Carolina Press, 1970.

Buxton, Julian T. III. *From Power to Poverty: A Description of Charleston, S.C. in the Years Immediately Before and After the Civil War*. 1982, Princeton University, Princeton, N.J. A paper submitted to the History Department in partial fulfillment of the requirements for a Bachelor of Arts degree.

Chesnut, Mary Boykin. *A Diary from Dixie*. New York: D. Appleton and Company, 1905.

Dickey, James. *The Whole Motion: Poems 1949–1992*. Middletown, Conn.: Wesleyan University Press, 1992.

Grace, John P. *Facts and Figures Concerning the Cooper River Bridge*. A promotional pamphlet published in 1930 by Cooper River Bridge, Inc.

Hill, Raymond Putnam. *My Family of Souls*. Jericho, N.Y.: Exposition Press, 1974.

Ladd, Joseph Brown. *The Literary Remains of Joseph Brown*

Ladd, *M.D.* Collected by Elizabeth Haskins. New York: H. C. Sleight, 1832.

Martin, Margaret Rhett. *Charleston Ghosts*. Columbia: University of South Carolina Press, 1963.

Middleton, Francis Kinloch. *Letters of Francis Kinloch Middleton*. Privately published.

Poston, Jonathan H. *The Buildings of Charleston*. Columbia: University of South Carolina Press, 1997.

Reid, Whitelaw. *After the War: A Southern Tour*. London: S. Low, Son and Co., 1886.

Rosen, Robert N. *Confederate Charleston*. Columbia: University of South Carolina Press, 1994.

Trowbridge, J. T. *The South: A Tour of its Battlefields and Ruined Cities*. New York: Arno Press, 1969.

ARTICLES

Bennett, John. *The News and Courier,* March 23, 1942. "Brilliant Young Charlestonian Lost Life Defending Mysterious Actress' Repute."

The News and Courier, February 25, 1946. "Ship Cuts Gap in Cooper River Bridge During Gale, Car Plunge is Reported."

The News and Courier, February 26, 1946. "Twisted Steel Is Probed for Car in Cooper."

————. "Entire Family May Have Been in Auto That Went Off Bridge."

Olsen, Norman Jr. "Charleston of the Spirits," *Preservation Progress,* Vol. XXXII, No 4, November, 1988.